TIGER TIGER
BURNING
BRIGHT

TIGER TIGER
BURNING
BRIGHT

A PLAY BY *Peter S. Feibleman*

THE WORLD PUBLISHING COMPANY

CLEVELAND AND NEW YORK

Published by The World Publishing Company
2231 West 110th Street, Cleveland 2, Ohio

Published simultaneously in Canada by
Nelson, Foster & Scott Ltd.

Library of Congress Catalog Card Number: 63-18585
First Edition

Some of the characters in this play first appeared in
Mr. Feibleman's novel A Place Without Twilight.

The photographs in this book are by Friedman-Abeles, Inc.

FOR JUDITH

Memory—that strange deceiver!
Who can trust her? How believe her—
While she hoards with equal care
The poor and trivial, rich and rare;
Yet flings away, as wantonly,
Grave fact and loveliest fantasy?
—WALTER DE LA MARE

TIGER TIGER BURNING BRIGHT *was first presented on Broadway by Oliver Smith and Roger L. Stevens at The Booth Theatre on December 22, 1962 with the following cast:*

MAMA	Claudia McNeil
CLARENCE MORRIS, her son, aged 23	Alvin Alley
DAN MORRIS, her younger son, aged 19	Al Freeman, Jr.
CILLE MORRIS, her daughter, aged 18	Ellen Holly
ADELAIDE SMITH, a friend of the family, aged 23	Diana Sands
DEACON SITTRE MORRIS, of the Riverview Baptist Church, in his late forties	Roscoe Lee Browne
CELESTE CHIPLEY, the girl who lives next door, aged 19	Cicely Tyson
DEWEY CHIPLEY, her brother, aged 21	Bobby Dean Hooks
MR. KERES, a white man in his late thirties	Paul Barry
SERGEANT JAMESON, a soldier	Robert Macbeth
FIRST NEIGHBOR	Janet MacLachlan
SECOND NEIGHBOR	Rudy Challenger

Directed by Joshua Logan

Production designed by Oliver Smith

Costumes by Lucinda Ballard

Lighting by Feder

Associate Producers Lyn Austin and Victor Samrock

The action takes place in the kitchen and back yard of Mama's house on the outskirts of New Orleans. The time is late August of the early Nineteen Fifties.

ACT ONE

SCENE 1: Seven o'clock on a Sunday morning.
SCENE 2: That night.

ACT TWO

Eight o'clock on a Sunday morning, three weeks later.

TIGER TIGER
BURNING
BRIGHT

The time is late summer of a year shortly after the start of the Korean War. The place is Mama's house and its back yard in a Negro poor district of "back-of-town" New Orleans.

The right half of the stage (all directions are given as from the stage) is the kitchen of Mama's house. It is a large kitchen, and has almost always been used as a living room, although the house contains a living room as well. Only the two back walls are visible, the other two suggested. The visible walls go up endlessly, out of sight. Their height is in total disproportion to anything else on the stage. They are like the wings of some gigantic bird, hovering; every object inside the kitchen is darkened by them; and the floor itself appears as a shadow of the walls. Also, it is important that the perspective of these walls be very slightly, and uniformly, distorted—and all of the furniture inside the kitchen angled in parallel distortion—to focus the audience's vision on the isolated heartbeat of the house: a framed telegram on the right wall, with a small shelf under it containing a pot of flowers and two of ivy—forming a kind of shrine. The lines of the kitchen must converge so completely on this small area that when the telegram is removed the distortion of the entire house becomes suddenly purposeless, meaningless, and therefore much more obvious. There is no noticeable color except for the telegram, the yellow of which stands out sharply from its black wood mourning frame. Yellow gleams through the glass of the frame, reflecting the lamplight so strongly that the glass seems to contain a light of its own.

13

The furniture of the kitchen is sparse in representation. There is a table, not much larger than a card table, set in the center of the room, or against the wall (depending on whether it is close to mealtime). There are four straight chairs, either at the table or scattered around, and a big wooden rocking chair, permanently down right. There are three doors: one leads off to the living room, the second to Clarence's room. The third, on the left (suggested) wall, leads onto the gallery and back yard. Below this door on the same wall are a low sink and cabinet, the outline of a window, and the suggestion of a mirror frame suspended in the air. The only real source of light is a large bulb hanging on an endless cord in the center of the room. Directly over the telegram on the wall there is also a small pipe-lamp of the kind used to illuminate paintings. This produces a hard halo of light, which is limited strictly in area; it is almost always on, even when the overhead bulb is turned off. Due to the enormity of the walls, most of the furniture seems a shade smaller than it would in a real house. Only the doors, the rocking chair, and the telegram are of sizes somewhat proportionate to the walls.

Outside, left, we see the end of the gray wood gallery, which soon runs out of sight along the length of the house. A few steps lead down from this to the ground. In the yard, next to the house and quite far downstage, is a long wooden bench, full of worm holes, and wet-looking. There is an oak tree all the way left, partly offstage; slats of wood have been built in a complete circle around it, to sit on—fixed to the trunk of the tree. The oak soars up with some attempt to balance the house in height, but only because it is a tall tree: nothing outside the house is in any way exaggerated, distorted, or untrue to reality. The yard and everything it contains is both realistic and simple. Several sad gray clotheslines connect separate points of the house to a single spike pushed into the tree—as if someone had tried once to prove that the two belonged together in the same world. In the middle, where the spike is placed, the oak is bent fur-

thest off; its roots and branches curve in toward the house. The great tree seems to be cringing away at the spot where the connecting clotheslines touch, unable in its last years to flourish as the house has grown—unwilling to serve as an anchor for such fearful expansion.

Between the tree and the house in the background we can see a cemetery, with a wall (or fence) and a black iron gate. In a semicircle on top of the gate the single word RIVERVIEW *is visible in large black iron grillwork. Through the gate we see a white path made of clamshells, curving out of sight.*

The brooding quality of Mama's house is due, as has been said, to dimension and color—but not to lack of light; rather it is enhanced by the effect of too much light coming from the one bulb at the center of the room, which throws shadows in every direction. When they strike the two walls, their effect is that of shadows against or within shadow. Mama's kitchen has been reconstructed to preserve her wishes and hopes. In it Reality seems like Fantasy, because Fantasy has become Reality. The house is a weatherproof stronghold for mildewed dreams. Yet it appears to us proud, strong—and even in a sense more solid than the oak tree to which it is attached. Not the house but the outside world (in juxtaposition, as we now see it) looks just a little bit peculiar.

And the same is true of all those from the real world who walk into Mama's house: they look peculiar. Except for Mama herself (whose physical dimensions are extraordinary), everyone seems somewhat off-kilter in the kitchen, as if he were too small, or walking at a wrong angle. She alone can match the size of the walls with her size—their distorted grandeur with her own—so that she appears to belong in any part of the room or any doorway she happens to use. Other people look wrong in the house. Especially her daughter Cille, pale and wraithlike, seems strange by contrast.

There may be two instruments used thematically in the

*play: the flute for Cille; the oboe for Mama. The flute is a
reminder of Reality. Its sound must accordingly be thin,
exact, and focused. The tune may wander, probing always
into new fields, new patterns and melodies of sound. Mama's
music, the oboe, is of a different kind, representative of
Fantasy. It plays a single melody which is repetitious
throughout—a lullaby which only completes and then repeats itself again, running in a set musical orbit around and
around the stage: thick, deep, wallowing, and thunderously
vague.*

Act One

Seven a.m. on a Sunday in late August.

Before Curtain, seven chimes from the church bell.

At Curtain, the stage is empty. The dawn sky over the graveyard is bleak and white, without any red. The only light in the kitchen is the one over the telegram which has been burning all night like a flame over an icon.

Clarence enters stealthily from the graveyard.

Clarence is known for his looks wherever he goes. His features are regular, more Caucasian than Negroid, with very light skin and particularly wide eyes. He is Mama's height, or taller; has a narrow waist and hips, long legs. He treats his physical appearance like something almost separate from him; protects it in the same way he would a slightly more perishable property than a thousand-dollar bill. He primps occasionally; he does not preen, and is never effeminate in speech or movement. The heavy noiselessness of his tread is cushioned within by muscles. He walks silently—lithe and smooth—never making a whisper of a sound. In Mama's house he walks with the controlled strength, the grace, the even

17

sway, and that sensual yet wholly neuter movement of a tiger wandering in its cage.

He glances once at kitchen, then goes behind house. Removes screen from the window of his room; climbs in, replaces screen. Then a radio is heard off left. He opens the living-room door, putting on his pajama top, and peers out; sees that the room is empty; runs across it quickly out to gallery. He shouts, "Turn that radio down: it's seven o'clock in the morning." Goes back through living room, but stops in front of the telegram as if he could not pass it. He touches it. He breaks past it and is about to go back into his room when Cille enters from living room.

Cille is thin, small, and in every way looks unlike Mama (who can darken a room merely by standing in front of the light). Cille seems at times transparent, and one has the feeling, were the light strong enough, she would become invisible. She is not at all "pretty." There is, however, a certain solemn dignity and peace about her—a quiet sensibility that can be mistaken for beauty.

CLARENCE

Is Mama awake?

CILLE

Yes.

He starts for his room.

Where have you been, Clarence?

CLARENCE

Been? I just got up.

CILLE

Simply.

Did you?

18

CLARENCE
After a slight pause. Chuckles.
You're beginning to ask more questions than she does.
Another pause.
She hasn't played the record yet, has she?

CILLE
No.

CLARENCE
Touches door. Laughs. Then with sudden violence.
The same goddam record every morning for fifteen years.
Sometimes I think if I hear it once more I'll . . . Who could
name a song "Thank God for a Garden"? There is no way of
living in this house.

*He exits. Cille watches after him for a moment,
then turns and exits slowly.*

Mama enters the kitchen from living room.

*Mama is very dark. She is enormous from any
angle. Her girth is exceeded only by her
height (which she uses to the fullest, never
stooping); the two dimensions look as right
together as Mama does in her house. She is
archetypal. The neighborhood children play
at guessing her weight; yet they do not think
of her as fat. It is said by adults that Mama
always looks smaller the second time you see
her, but from then on begins to grow. She is
not flabby, and she doesn't waddle. She rocks.
She is known around this part of town simply as "a great big woman."*

*She begins the day by checking the house
clock, winding it. Then she peers out window
at sky directly over house; clucks affrontedly.
Lights burner under coffeepot. Goes to sideboard, takes out phonograph, winds it. Takes
out record. Sits at table. Plays "Thank God for*

*a Garden" very loud. The music continues
and Mama does not move.*

*Dan comes in from living room, wearing pa-
jamas, sleepy-faced, his hair tousled.*

*Dan is the ugly one of Mama's children. What
has come to be known among them as their
"no-colored color" is sallow on him, and a little
too yellow. His face is thin and his nose too
flat. His body is what people call "shapeless";
and in further contrast to his brother, Dan is
awkward in each movement, and equally awkward when he does not move. He is shy and
hides behind his eyes: he is a very private person. He has nothing in common with Cille or
Clarence except this sense of privateness.*

Cille comes in, sits quietly beside Dan.

*Clarence enters last from his bedroom.
Stretches, catlike; sits next to Cille. They all
remain motionless while the record plays
through. This is a ritual of every morning. Dan
and Cille are without expression. Mama's face
is ecstatic. Clarence's expression is one of total
disgust.*

*At end, Cille and Dan rise, kiss Mama. They
both say "good morning" to her and exit. Clarence sits without moving.*

CLARENCE
Quietly incredulous.
Don't you honestly get tired of that record, Mama?

MAMA
Some people still say good morning. In the morning.

CLARENCE
Some people still don't have to wake up nauseated.

20

MAMA
You and them big book words.

CLARENCE
It means . . .

MAMA
I know what it means. You going to?

CLARENCE
Fast.
I will if you put that record back on. "Thank God for a Garden."

MAMA
Since when don't I play it through twice? If you going to get any sudden objections about my record, you best go back to bed again.

CLARENCE
No, Mama. I never had a sudden objection to anything. Except getting born.

MAMA
You want your coffee?

CLARENCE
Yeah.

MAMA
Yeah ain't no proper answer.

CLARENCE
Passing a hand over his face.
Yes, please, Mama, I would surely enjoy some coffee.

MAMA
All right then.
Cille enters, starts to work.
Mama calls.
Daniel, did you wash up yet? I got something to do in the living room.

CLARENCE

What on earth are you fixing the living room up for, Mardi Gras?

MAMA

None of your business what for.

> *Clarence exits. To Cille. Tensely and uneasily.*

I done made up my mind. We are going to have the surprise party for him—tonight. Just like I planned.

CILLE

Are we, Mama?

MAMA

I plain don't like the way your brother's walking around my house lately. Just walking around. Making silence. Waiting for his draft notice. It's time Clarence remembered how much he is respected here at home. That is the point of the party.

CILLE

> *Quietly; simply.*

I don't think it will work, Mama.

MAMA

With outsiders and everything, just like he used to beg me when he was . . . What you talking about now?

> *Cille makes a movement with her hands in front of her eyes.*

And don't start with that scratching at the air. Whenever you don't believe something I say you does that. You know what happens when you gets a new habit with your eyes.

CILLE

I'm sorry, Mama.

> *Resumes work.*

MAMA

This is a time for happiness. I don't understand what's going on in my house these days.

> *Goes out to gallery. Takes clothes in off line.*

> *Clarence comes into kitchen, sits at table, sips coffee.*

There's a little bitty cloud sitting up over the kitchen.

CILLE
> *Following Mama.*

Where?

MAMA

Right there. I hope it don't rain for tonight. You better tell it to get off.

CILLE

I don't know how, Mama.

MAMA

What you mean, you don't know how? Just tell it, that's all. I never did see such a houseful of helpless children in my life.
> *Speaks to the cloud angrily.*

Get off of there. Go on, I said. Get off.
> *Stalks past Cille to the clothesbasket.*

DAN
> *Opens living-room door.*

I washed my face.

CLARENCE

Congratulations.

DAN

I was talking to Mama.

CLARENCE

She's not here.

MAMA
> *Coming in from gallery, followed by Cille.*

Yes, I am. Go and try on that old suit of Clarence's, lamb. I might have to take it in a little.

CLARENCE

What's he want to put a suit on today for?

MAMA

Never you mind what for.
                    Slight pause.
What you looking at?

CLARENCE

Nothing, nothing, nothing.

MAMA
                    Tensely.
Tiger cat. You run your eyes at me. Only you ain't going to
upset me today. *Not today.*

CLARENCE

What's today?

MAMA

Nothing.
                    Pointing to Cille, who is ironing.
Look at your sister. Happy as a bird. Why can't you be like
her?

CLARENCE

How can a cat be like a bird?

MAMA

And don't start to heckle me. I only just put myself in a
good mood again. I got to go open up the living-room table
for tonight.

CLARENCE

Who ever eats in the living room?

MAMA

We do: sometimes. On very special occasions.
                    Clarence doesn't answer.
Your Uncle Sittre Morris is back from one of his monthly
trips. And Adelaide will be here and . . .

CLARENCE

Oh, my God.

MAMA

Don't you swear.

CLARENCE

Adelaide.

MAMA

Adelaide just happens to be a fine girl; and your brother
Daniel is in love with her.

CLARENCE

God knows why.

MAMA

Do you hear me? You shut your dirty mouth. And keep it
shut until it opens clean. I see things the way I see them,
and the way I see them is, and was, and is going to be the
way they are seen around here. This is still my house.

CLARENCE

It will always be your house, Mama.

DAN

*Enters, in a pair of trousers too large and
baggy.*

I got the pants on.

CLARENCE

So we see.

DAN

Will you please comb my hair?

CLARENCE

Will I what?

MAMA

Give it here.
Combs Dan's hair.
I'll take them trousers in later.

CLARENCE

Nineteen years old, he can't comb his own hair?

MAMA

Defensively.

He can. He just don't like to. The mirror scares him.

CLARENCE

Since when?

MAMA

Since at least a month. He says he don't see hisself no more.

CLARENCE

Who do you see . . . Shakespeare?

MAMA

Watch your language.

CLARENCE

Don't you get upset. I always forget you think Shakespeare's alive.

MAMA

Who are you today? I don't think nothing. I know he's a book. I sleeps with him under my bed, don't I? Well? Don't I?

CLARENCE

Only because you didn't know what else to do with those books when father died.

MAMA

I sleeps with him under my bed, and I sleeps like a baby. Mr. William Shakespeare don't upset me one little bit. Him or no other friend of your father's.

To Dan.

You look real nice. Go on in and open up that table for me.

Dan goes out.

You look nice too.

CLARENCE

Thank you.

26

MAMA

Look at that: a fingerprint. Who touched my telegram?
*Clarence recoils slightly. Mama takes telegram
down and polishes glass with her apron during the following.*
I wish I understood the way you acting . . . ever since they
announced that war in Korea. Eight years you been working for the telegraph company. Eight whole years. And I
remember every single day.

CLARENCE

Averting his eyes.
Tell me a day you remember, Mama.

MAMA

The day you brought me this. When you was only a delivery
boy. It took a man to walk in that door and read this out
loud to his mother's face. "The Government of the United
States regrets to inform you of the death of your son, George
Morris . . ." Yes, sir, you acted like a man. Even before
then. From the day your papa passed away . . .

CLARENCE

He didn't. You can't drink yourself to death and "pass
away." Papa only died.

MAMA

What's wrong with my using a nice pretend word instead of
a real one? What would you want me to say? Your papa
was a sinner? Laying out there under that tree . . . reading
them books and practicing that ridiculous music on his
flute. I saved his soul, but not because he wanted me to.
"Nora," he'd say, "do anything you wish with me. Hit me.
Slap me. Bust my flute. But for God's sake don't save me."
Yes, you laugh. The Lord will teach you to laugh.

CLARENCE

He already has, Mama; He already has done that.
Cille goes out.
Cille has a new habit.

MAMA

Uneasily.

Your sister gets a new one every month with her eyes, she's got a sickness, that's all.

CLARENCE

Sickness? She can't see anything but the truth. That's what you mean by sick, not her headaches: that's how she got the headaches. That's why she scares you.

MAMA

Scares who? How do you sound, what is this special talk . . .

DAN

Running through from living room.

Here she comes. Adelaide . . . *Adelaide* . . .

CLARENCE

Oh, Lord.

MAMA

Where you going?

> *Clarence exits to bedroom, shuts door. Mama hangs the telegram as Adelaide enters yard. Adelaide is tall, slender, exquisitely shaped; long and thin and bone-lovely, with tiny wrists, and fingers and gestures that never seem to end. She speaks with an affectedly liquid voice, which she conserves as though she were afraid her supply might end. She does everything slowly, with carefully doled-out energy. Her dress is black and is accompanied by a large black filmy picture hat and a black parasol to keep the sun off. She acts as though she carried the weight of the world, although in truth she has dismissed it. She would seem to be in mourning for herself.*

> *Dan has run outside.*

DAN
Showing off his trousers.
For the party.

ADELAIDE
Shhhh. Don't mention the party. It's supposed to be a surprise.

MAMA
Blossoming.
Is that you out there, Adelaide?

ADELAIDE
Why, yes, I believe it is. Right out here under the heat of day. Just wilting.

DAN
What, doing what?

ADELAIDE
Wilting.

DAN
You hear what she said, Mama? Like a flower, understand? Just . . .

ADELAIDE
Daniel, *please.* What a unnecessary explanation.
To Mama, who comes outside and kisses her.
I was never so surprised as when Daniel come running over last night to say you-all are having an occasion. I got so excited I just went and dyed another one of my mama's dresses black for tonight. Not this one, a party dress. As you know, I wouldn't appear here in anything but black.

DAN
Why not, Adelaide?

ADELAIDE
Why, what a silly question. Because of your brother George, of course. This is a house of bereavement. My papa was the only one who liked this color. He used to call it "classic" black.

29

To Mama, coyly.
I sometimes wonder why I am the only person you allow in
your house.

MAMA
Well you can stop wondering right now. I consider you one
of my children. I have . . . sort of adopted you . . . you
might say. For my son Daniel.
She starts inside.

ADELAIDE
Following on Mama's heels.
That's exactly what I tell people when they ask. I say,
Mrs. Morris has sort of adopted me. For her son Daniel.
To Dan, hard.
Ain't that what I say?
She goes inside.

DAN
Yes.

ADELAIDE
Your telegram looks just lovely this morning. Specially in
that light.

MAMA
Is your stomach all right today, Adelaide?

ADELAIDE
Now you mustn't ask me questions like that on a joyful day
like this. I can't help being delicate. I felt as if I had butter-
flies flittering through me when I got up. From the feeling
here.
*Puts three fingers over her stomach. Looks
around.*
Well, where is the man of the house? Where *is* he?

MAMA
In his room.
To Dan.
Maybe Adelaide would like a glass of cool water.

30

DAN

Yes, ma'am, with ice in it. With . . .

ADELAIDE

Ice? Daniel, ice? In *my* stomach?

MAMA

He forgot.

ADELAIDE

Stomach . . . is one of my least favorite words, and as fate would have it, it is the one I most have to use. Ever since my mama . . . passed beyond . . .

> *Dan presents her with glass on plate. Surprised.*

No, thank you. No water.

MAMA

Daniel is going to play on his trumpet for us tonight.

ADELAIDE

> *To Dan.*

It's about time.

> *To Mama.*

I mean I never heard him play.

> *Clarence enters quietly from bedroom.*

MAMA

> *To Adelaide.*

Maybe you and Daniel will walk with me. I got to get some special flowers for tonight.

ADELAIDE

Why, we'd be glad to. Wouldn't we, Daniel? Anything at all to alleviate the surprise.

CLARENCE

Surprise?

MAMA

Clarence. Sneaking around the house like that. I plain can't hear you walk these days.

31

CLARENCE

Sorry, Mama. I'll try to press down.

ADELAIDE

Gracious goodness. Good morning, Clarence. And happy occasion.

CLARENCE

Occasion of what?

ADELAIDE

Oh . . . just happy occasion.

CLARENCE

Thank you. And good morning.
Goes back into bedroom and closes door.

ADELAIDE

That was quick.

DAN

He must of forgot something.

ADELAIDE

He always does. Forget something. Do you mind if I fan myself?

MAMA

Please. Fan yourself.
Whispers.
I baked him a great big cake. He got another raise last month.

ADELAIDE

Why, if your son gets just one more promotion from the telegraph company I believe I will just faint.
Titters.

MAMA

Now what is in this mysterious gift-wrapped package?

ADELAIDE

Two hand-embroidered handkerchiefs. From the collection my mama was embroidering, after she got the Virulent

Diabetes. I only wish everyone could have a collection like that to draw on. Every orphan.

MAMA

You shouldn't of. Tell her, Daniel.

DAN

You shouldn't of.

ADELAIDE

I'm afraid Clarence won't agree with you. He'll probably just say, "Not another embroidered handerchief."

MAMA

No he won't, Clarence wouldn't say a thing like that.
Calls.
Clarence.
He opens door.
Adelaide brought you a present.

CLARENCE

Not another embroidered handkerchief.
Dully.
Thank you.
Closes door.

ADELAIDE
Rising. Annoyed.
Maybe we'd better be going. We wouldn't want to spoil his day. I hope I'll be feeling well enough to come this evening.

MAMA

But you got to: I invited the neighbors and . . .

ADELAIDE
Neighbors?
Stops short.
Why . . . you don't mean a *outside* party? After all these years? Well. This might be a even bigger surprise than I thought.
To Cille, who enters.
Don't you worry, sugar. We'll keep things quiet, the same as always; for both our sakes. My condition and your spells.

33

CILLE

I get headaches, Adelaide. Not spells.

ADELAIDE

Headaches. Just headaches. Of course.
To Mama.
Daniel and I will wait for you in the cemetery.
Goes out with Dan.
I do hate the heat in this city. I don't think a well-
brought-up person ever approves of the weather, do you?
My mama used to say, "The weather in New Orleans is
peculiar, even for weather." When are we what we are,
Daniel, in the summer or the winter?

DANIEL

I don't know.
Adelaide looks at him hopelessly. They exit.

CLARENCE
Opens bedroom door.

Did she go?

MAMA
Heavily.

She went.
Clarence comes in.
I don't understand how you can treat that girl like that.

CLARENCE

I don't treat the girl at all, Mama. She's your friend, not
mine.

MAMA

Adelaide ain't my friend. She is going to be married to
Daniel.

CLARENCE

Has he asked her yet?

MAMA

He will.

34

CLARENCE
Looks at her.
I see what you mean.

MAMA
You don't like anybody these days. Her or your uncle. Deacon Sittre Morris is your own father's brother; and he is the representative of God in my house.

CLARENCE
God? God.
He exits to living room.

MAMA
Staring after him.
Can't even look me in the eye for longer than a second.

CILLE
Quietly.
He'll be drafted soon. Maybe he wants to leave before that.

MAMA
Uneasily.
Why would he want to leave before?

CILLE
After a slight pause.
I don't know yet. I'll find out, Mama.

MAMA
Hard.
Don't find out nothing.

CILLE
I just want to know the truth.

MAMA
You leave the truth alone where it belongs. I know my son. He won't want to go away from me long as I keep him happy.
Sharply.
You do your work, that's all.

35

She looks at her.
And stop thinking. It makes me nervous.

CILLE

I'm sorry, Mama.

MAMA

You can just go on and get that ironing done.
Takes pie from oven and goes out to yard.

CILLE

Yes, Mama.
Mama exits through gates. Clarence enters.

CLARENCE
To Cille.
Where did she go?

CILLE

For roses.

CLARENCE

To put under there. Roses, my Lord. She must have been
talking about George again.

CILLE

This is August, Clarence. George left us in August.

CLARENCE

Did he? That's right. August.

CILLE

George ran away when Mama was asleep. He broke the
lock and . . .

CLARENCE

How would you know what he did? You were a kid. You
didn't even wake up.

CILLE

Mama had to have the lock repaired.

CLARENCE

Oh. That's right.

36

CILLE
Simply.
Why don't you do it the same way?

CLARENCE
Why don't I . . . That's—
He turns away.
—a crazy idea.

CILLE
Then how will you leave?

CLARENCE
I'm not ever leaving.

CILLE
You passed your physical last week. You'll be drafted soon . . .

CLARENCE
I'll think of a way to get out of the draft.

CILLE
Why, Clarence? Why can't you leave here?
Slowly.
Is there something Mama might find out . . . if you left?

CLARENCE
Sister, maybe you'd better tend to your own life.

CILLE
Simply.
I don't have a life.

CLARENCE
Be glad of that.
He exits.

Celeste Chipley enters the yard, beckons to her brother Dewey, who follows.

Celeste is a pleasant-faced girl who is composed entirely of small circles and ovals. There is not a hollow in her body. She is a touch too

37

*gaudy in her dress and make-up, though not
at all vulgar. Dewey is a handsome boy who
has not quite yet outgrown the shock of being
born.*

CELESTE
Calls.

Cille? Lucille?
Pushes past her into house.

CILLE

Hello, Celeste.

CELESTE

How come you knew my name?

CILLE

I've seen you next door.

CELESTE

My, what a . . . dark kitchen.
Too tentatively.
Is your mama home?

CILLE

No.

DEWEY

Good morning, Lucille.
*Stands awkwardly, holding a bunch of flowers,
unable to present them to her.*

CELESTE
Examining the kitchen curiously.

You acquainted with my brother Dewey: assistant druggist
at Nash's drugstore? I was lying just now. I knew your
mama was out. Saw her walking into Riverview Cemetery
with a fresh pie a few seconds ago.

CILLE

Yes.

38

CELESTE

Carries a fresh pie through that old cemetery every week.

CILLE

Yes.

CELESTE

Edging toward living room.

When the deacon telephoned yesterday to say we might be invited to a party here, I like to collapsed. I mean . . . I just came over to help with the preparations.

Looks at her.

That's a lie, too.

CILLE

I know.

CELESTE

I been looking for an excuse to get in here ever since we moved next door. This the living room?

Throws open door. A slight pause.

Nothing but furniture, huh? Say . . . Do you mind if I ask a personal question?

CILLE

I don't mind.

CELESTE

Where do you keep the cadaver?

CILLE

We don't have one.

CELESTE

But they say . . .

CILLE

They say we put the cadaver away before we allow anybody in the house. We don't, Celeste. We can't. We don't have one.

CELESTE

God damn it. What a shame.

CILLE

I'm sorry.

DEWEY

I told her it was only gossip, but Sister was anxious to see for herself.

CELESTE

What do you mean, *Sister* was anxious . . .

CILLE

I understand.

CELESTE

Say, do you always know when people are lying?

CILLE

I think so.

CELESTE

Do you always tell the truth yourself?

CILLE

Yes.

CELESTE

Jesus, what a creepy place. How come your mama won't allow anybody in here . . . except for the deacon and that Adelaide Smith girl?

DEWEY

Her mama just doesn't like strangers.

CELESTE

You bringing me news.
To Cille.
You know . . . you seem kind of natural to me. I mean, the way everybody talks . . . I thought you were a little . . . well . . . odd.

DEWEY

I told you she looked normal at the drugstore.

40

CELESTE

Why do you always wear that same dress?

CILLE

I only have one kind of dress.

CELESTE

You could get in your slip during the day . . .

CILLE

Mama wouldn't let me around the house like that.

CELESTE

In a slip? In New Orleans? What's the matter, don't she ever
go to the movies?
Points.
I knew there was something strange. What you got a telegram on the wall for? Now that's the silliest thing I ever
saw.
Giggles. Reads.
"The Government of the United States regrets to inform
you of the death . . ." Oh. I apologize. I didn't know.

DEWEY

Sister.

Clarence enters. Celeste backs up.

CLARENCE

What are you people doing here?

DEWEY

We . . . just . . .

CLARENCE
To Cille.
You let them in.

DEWEY

She didn't let us, we walked in.

CELESTE

Your mama invited us.

CLARENCE

What?

CELESTE

To the party. Tonight.

CLARENCE

What party? What is she talking about?

CILLE

I promised not to tell you.

DEWEY

Sister.

CELESTE

Oh, Lord.

CLARENCE

All right. I'll talk to Mama about it later.
            To Celeste and Dewey.
You just get out. Both of you.
            Exits.

CELESTE
            To Dewey.
He's the one goes crawling out his bedroom window in the
middle of the night.

DEWEY

You better keep your mouth shut.

CELESTE

She must know, they live in the same house.

CILLE

No. I didn't know.

CELESTE

This is the strangest place I ever been in.
            *Mama enters from cemetery; Dewey sees her,
            snaps his fingers.*
What are you snapping your fingers for?
            She sees Mama and gasps. A pause.

42

DEWEY

Dewey and Celeste Chipley, ma'am.

MAMA

Chipley?

DEWEY

From next door.
A slight pause.

MAMA
Tonelessly.

Next door?

CELESTE

Right there. The name is on the mailbox. Chipley. You must be familiar with the name.

MAMA

No. I'm not familiar with the name.

DEWEY

But . . . but you invited us for this evening. Deacon Sittre called and said . . .

MAMA

Oh.
Formally.
You must excuse me. We are not used to visitors. We have not had many. Since the wake for my son George.

CELESTE

No'm.

CLARENCE
Enters.

Mama . . .

MAMA
Hard.
You are acquainted with my son Clarence? He works for the telegraph company.

CELESTE

Yes'm. I'm afraid we spoiled the surprise.

43

MAMA

That's all right. The party is in his honor.

CLARENCE

There isn't going to be any party.

MAMA

Yes, there is. He always wanted one. He always begged me—

CLARENCE
To the Chipleys.
I asked you to get out of here.

MAMA
To Celeste.
I see you are watching my telegram. You have tears in your eyes.

CELESTE

Cornflowers.

MAMA

What?

CELESTE

I'm allergic.

DEWEY
Still trying to give the flowers to Cille.
To these.

MAMA
Taking them.
It was kind of you to bring me flowers. Thank you.

DEWEY

But I . . .

MAMA

Yes?

Dewey shrugs and looks confused.

CELESTE
Covering for him.
What pretty roses.

44

MAMA

From the Reverend at the church. Every week I bake a pie
for him, and he gives me fresh flowers to put under my
telegram. We don't have any flowers left in our garden. Our
garden is all used up.

CELESTE

You don't say.

MAMA

I used to have my own garden in Atlanta. I come from Atlanta. I can't seem to make nothing grow in this flat land.

DEWEY

Have you tried fertilizer?
    Mama stares at him.

CELESTE

I knew it wasn't true what they claim.

MAMA

What who claim?

CELESTE

Well, I . . . that is, the grocer's new wife heard those stories
about you-all . . .

MAMA

She just had to repeat them, too. Some people plain have to
whisper.

CELESTE

Yes'm.

MAMA

Always. Always. Well? I suppose you waiting for me to ask
what she said. You think I care to hear what that fresh
woman said?

CELESTE

No'm, I . . .

MAMA

What did she say?

People call you Mother of the World because you are a great big woman. And you-all can't have visitors because Cille is peculiar.

MAMA

Go on.

CELESTE

Your son Clarence is the most handsome man around New Orleans. And your apple pies are so bad you have to go out and bury them yourself in the graveyard.

MAMA

We will expect you this evening.

CLARENCE

No. We will not.

DEWEY
To Mama.
Thank you for the invitation.

CLARENCE

There is no invitation.

MAMA

There is now.

CLARENCE

The invitation is canceled.

MAMA

We are going to have a party: that is my last word on the subject.

DEWEY

Come on, Sister.
They leave.

CLARENCE
Waits until they are out of sight. Tensely.
Listen, Mama . . .

46

MAMA

Listen nothing. Tiger, tiger, tiger cat. First you snarl at Adelaide, now the neighbors. You act like this house was your own private cage.

CLARENCE

It is.

MAMA
To Cille.

Leave us alone.

CILLE

But, Mama . . .

MAMA

Leave us. Go on outside and get some air. Breathing is a thing you never did too much of: that's how come you gets winded so easily. Just sit under that oak tree. *And breathe.*
Cille goes out to yard and sits under tree.
So. You found out, satisfied?

CLARENCE
Harshly.

Mama. We've never had a party before. Not even on a birthday . . . And this isn't anybody's . . .

MAMA

It is a pretend birthday if I say it is. A pretend party.

CLARENCE
Echoes.

A pretend party.
He begins to laugh helplessly.

MAMA

Is this what you got out of all them reading books? To laugh? To act like this?
He goes on laughing.
A little listening might teach you to be a little more like your brother George.

47

CLARENCE
Stops laughing. Suddenly, viciously polite.
Might it? More dead, you mean, Mama? Or just blacker?

MAMA
After a slight pause. Low.
Ask me that again. I said ask me that again.
Dan enters and comes to door.
Daniel, we are having a private discussion. Go on and sit
out there and help your sister breathe.
Dan joins Cille at tree.
You go and rest then. Go then. Go on. Go.
*Takes telegram down, dissatisfied. Repolishes
it.*
But I'm having my party for you just the same.

CLARENCE
Mama, there's no such thing as a pretend party. There are
only real parties. With real people. People who ask questions. You can't afford to have anybody nosing around here,
there are too many secrets.

MAMA
I don't have any secrets in my house.

CLARENCE
Don't you? You're talking to one right now. Mama, how long
have you been pretending?

MAMA
Turning away.
I don't know what you're talking about. I was even going to
give you a present myself.

CLARENCE
Then give me the truth.

MAMA
The truth? It was you gave that to me.
Holds telegram up between them.
This here is the . . .

48

CLARENCE

Mama, will you for God's sake put that telegram down?

MAMA

Don't you swear. I'll put it up. I'll put it up, not down.
Hangs telegram on wall.
Did you find the truth in them books you read, or working
for the telegraph company? There is only the one that be-
longs to the Lord, and the one in here,
Her heart.
and that one up there.
The telegram.
If you can think of any other truth, I wish you to tell it to
me now.

CLARENCE

All right, Mama. One more.
A slight pause. Then tonelessly.
I don't work for the telegraph company.

MAMA
Frowns. Dully.

You what?

CLARENCE
*The same toneless voice: he remains the same
for the rest of scene.*
I don't work for the telegraph company.

MAMA

What do you mean by that?
He doesn't answer.
You don't *work* for them. Clarence, don't you be teasing me
today. Course you work for the . . .

CLARENCE

I don't work for the telegraph company.

MAMA

Stop teasing with me, what do you mean? Where . . .
where was you working when you brought me that?

49

CLARENCE

I worked for them then.

MAMA

For them *then*? And since when don't you work for them?

CLARENCE

Since then.

MAMA

You . . . stop joking with me, Clarence.
Backs a step away.
Stop . . . looking at me that way, I don't believe you. You
mean to tell me they . . . fired you . . . seven years ago?

CLARENCE

No. They didn't fire me.

MAMA

Scared; groping for quick proof.
And what about them people who send for you all the time,
always say right away first thing they're from the telegraph
company. And that white lady, that Mrs. Soren . . . came
here looking for you last month? Told me her husband was
the president of the company. What about her? Was that
the truth?

CLARENCE

Yes.

MAMA

Her husband is the president?

CLARENCE

He is the vice-president.

MAMA

Pouncing.
And she came here to find you. Her, the president's wife
herself, and she told me personally . . . Clarence, I said you
stop looking at me that way . . . She told me personally how
much she valued you. And how about all them raises you

50

been getting, and the money you bring home; and where do you go at night then, all dressed up, after you said they put you on the evening shift?

Clarence doesn't answer.

She told me personally, that Mrs. Soren . . . *She told me personally* . . . how much she valued you. Now you tell me again you don't work for the telegraph company.

CLARENCE

I don't work for the telegraph company.

MAMA

I don't believe it. You are joking with me, I don't believe you. You're playing games with your old mama here, Clarence, you got no right. Stop it.

Guttural.

Stop it, Clarence.

Desperately.

Please. Stop it.

CLARENCE

The same voice.

All right, Mama. I was only teasing.

MAMA

You . . .

A slight pause. Laughs.

I knew it, I knew that all the time. Did you think you had your old mama fooled? Twenty-three years of age and still likes to play games on his mama.

CLARENCE

Games.

Facing the yard.

Look now. Look at that place out there.

Turns to face her, pointing.

Take a look at it. You kept the world out of this house for as old as I am. Now you think you can invite it to a party?

MAMA

Who says I can't?

51

I do. It's too late now. You've been afraid for too long, Mama.
Afraid, afraid . . .

MAMA
Confronting him.
Yes. I was afraid. But do you know what of?

CLARENCE
The world out there. The whole world . . .

MAMA
Much more than the world. I was afraid of the night and the
day. Of the light in your sister's eyes. I was even afraid of
your color, don't you know that? I was afraid you would
have to pay for my mistake.

Once there was a woman, sitting in her house . . .
Points to rocker.
Sitting in that chair, and rocking a little black baby that
matched the color of her arms. And this woman couldn't
tell where her own body stopped and where the baby's be-
gan. Because they was the same, same thing, the two of
them. And then something else come to happen to her. She
had another baby. And another, and another. She had three
more babies. Can you remember the whispering around my
house? While you slept at night and after . . . great whole
voices without sound . . . could you ever feel it there? No,
sir. Because I never let you. Because I kept the door locked
till you was big enough to make you a place . . . till you
couldn't tell the whispers from the wind.

I come from Atlanta. I don't come from here. I come from
Atlanta. And your papa came to visit and he brought me
here. They warned me against him. They said he would
drink and dream and fade on me—but I spit in my own father's face, and I left my home. I married the stranger and
I went with him. Do you know the difference between New
Orleans and Atlanta? Do you know the change from there
to here? This is a swampland place. This land is flat, and wet
and dark, without no red; and flat, and flat, and flat. No

rolling and no hills. No place for the sun to go at the end of the day. But in Atlanta when the day ends . . . between the red hills and the red earth . . . there at one edge of the world is a place for the sun to die. And the color it makes there, dying . . . You know the name of that color? They call that color twilight.

It is the softest, the most beautiful color I have ever seen.
She touches Clarence's skin.
It is the color of dreams. I loved it so much . . . I even married a man who carried that color in his body. Only I didn't know . . . till later years I didn't even think I could of married him just for that reason alone. But the Lord knew. And He punished me. Because the man I married took me to a place to live . . . he took me to this swampland place . . . to live . . . and to bear him his children. And when I got off the train here; the first day here . . . I hadn't ever seen a place so flat. I had never in my life seen a place so flat it didn't have one hill and one valley to rock down the sun; to cradle it in at the end of the day. He brought me here to live, he brought me here. And he *died* here. And left me with my children. In a place like this. What can you do in a place without no twilight?
Passionately.
I'll tell you what I did. In case you don't remember now, I'll tell you. I took in washing. And I let my two oldest . . . I let you and George go out on the street and work, because I didn't have no other choice; because we needed the money. And I washed and washed and I washed. Through twenty-seven payments on this house, and I'm still washing. And every time you went out to work I shook so bad I was afraid you would feel it in the floor. Not for your black brother George, no. *I only shook for my guilt. I shook for my beautiful dream.* I shook for you. But I never let you know. I made up stories and pretends; I kept my hands on the wet laundry, and I used my shaking to wash with. And whenever I could, in every single way I ever could, I kept my babies out of that world. I did. Yes, I did. All my babies.

And then one night, your brother George couldn't stand it any more, and he broke out and ran away. Do you think I didn't know he left because of me? Do you think I didn't hold my stomach and vomit, and cry to God to keep that child from becoming a criminal? Until I knew he was safe. Until I knew he had done the right thing and gone in the service of his country. Until you brought me that. Yes, yes, yes, I was afraid.

But I ain't now. I did the things I did: those things are done. And if there is any other way I should of done them, or any better way I should of lived, then you tell it to me now, Mr. Book Man. Please tell me right now. I don't come from here. I come from Atlanta.

CURTAIN

Act One

SCENE 2

Seven o'clock that night. The house is full of a thick, amber-red glow, which must contrast so with the night that the two areas—inside and outside the house—seem like different worlds. The backdrop: the bleak sky over the graveyard is an empty dark blue, illuminated only by the dead white light of the moon.

Cille is alone in the kitchen taking out dessert plates and setting them on the sideboard. The door to the living room is shut, and sounds of the party are heard: laughing, talking, the chinking of plates. Dan is heard trying to play a tune on the trumpet.

Mama enters, closes door; crosses past birthday cake. Stops, stares at the candle.

MAMA

I don't care what the grocer done said. It still looks like a thermometer to me.

CILLE

It's supposed to, Mama. They call it a Century Candle.

MAMA

I don't care what they calls it.

CILLE

It's got a hundred years marked on the side.

MAMA

Clarence ain't no hundred years old. He is exactly twenty-three and a half. I sends you out for twenty-three and a half little candles and you come back with one big thermometer. Don't give the right tone for a celebration. Gives the tone for sickness. Puts me in mind of the measles.

I wonder what's keeping your uncle. We got to wait on the cake and the singing till he gets here.

Does that Celeste Chipley and her brother have singing voices?

CILLE

I don't know, Mama. I don't see why not.

MAMA

She don't seem like such a bad girl. She had tears in her eyes . . . from looking at my telegram.

CILLE

She had a sniffle, Mama.

MAMA

Now there you goes again, you see? Imagining things.

CILLE

I didn't imagine it. It's just the naked truth.

MAMA

Well, dress it up a little. I don't want nothing naked in my house.

Dewey enters. Stops when he sees Mama.

DEWEY

Oh, I thought maybe I could . . .

MAMA

Could what?

DEWEY

Lamely.

Help . . . with something.

MAMA

In a kitchen? A man?

SITTRE

In cemetery. Trips over grave.
God damn it to hell.
Calls out to Mama.
Good evening, Sister Nora.

MAMA

There you is, Deacon. How are you?

SITTRE

Enters. Deacon Sittre is a well-groomed, nice-looking man dressed as a minister.
I tripped over a grave.
He rubs his shin.

MAMA

Did you hurt yourself?

SITTRE

I can't pass along there like you do in the dark.
To Cille.
Your mama just tears through that cemetery like there was no tomorrow.

MAMA

To Dewey.
My husband always used to say: there are only two ways to leave this house. The cemetery or the railroad station.

DEWEY

Conversationally.
Which way did he use?
Mama stares at him. He exits.

MAMA

To Cille.
Say hello to Uncle Sittre. He just got back from another of his doing-good trips.

To Sittre.
I don't know where you gets the money to do so many good deeds.

SITTRE
Good evening, Lucille.
> *Cille draws back from him; turns away.*

MAMA
She never was much for talking.

SITTRE
How is Clarence getting along?

MAMA
He got a four-hundred-dollar bonus only last week, and . . .

SITTRE
Four hundred dollars . . .
> *Exits to living room.*

MAMA
> *Picks up cake. To Cille.*
Here we go now. You carry them plates. And remember to start singing if they don't.
> *Looking at the cake, she starts to sing "He's Got the Whole World in His Hands." She exits, Cille following. There is applause off-stage, then the others join in the singing.*
>
> *During the singing, Keres appears in the yard. He is a weak-looking white man, unhappy and limp in the summer. He goes to gallery, peers into kitchen. He ducks away as Cille comes into the kitchen. She is followed by Clarence.*

CILLE
Go on back. I'll get it.

CLARENCE
> *Uneasily.*
The heat's getting worse. Feels like the house is breathing in.

58

CILLE
To Clarence at window.
What do you keep looking for out there?

CLARENCE
Nobody. I mean nothing.

CILLE
Where do you go at night, Clarence?

CLARENCE
No place, Miss Questionnaire.
Quickly.
Sister, I love you. Just don't get too curious about me.
Evasively.
Look. I got a party present for Mama. She never had any
jewelry.
Holds them up.

CILLE
Where did you get those earrings?

CLARENCE
At a shop, where do you think? I went to a store after I finished work yesterday and . . .

CILLE
You can't stop lying, can you? Mama won't let you stop.
What *is* your work, Clarence?

SITTRE
Enters from living room.
Congratulations on your four-hundred-dollar bonus, Clar-
ence.

CLARENCE
After a slight pause. Flat.
What do you want, Uncle Sittre? I lent you twenty dollars
last month.

SITTRE
Smoothly.

59

It seems I need to *borrow* about twice that much. This
month.

> *Clarence gives him money.*

And don't look down your nose at me, Clarence.

> *To Cille.*

He always disapproves of my little innocent vices. I like to
play the horses now and then. Is there something so wrong
with that?

CILLE

There's something wrong with telling Mama you visit church
parishes.

SITTRE

> *Looking at Clarence.*

I'm not the only one who makes up stories for your mama.
Thank you, Clarence. Let me know if you get any more
bonuses.

> *He exits.*

CILLE

He makes you give him money all the time, doesn't he?
Why do you let him?

CLARENCE

I'll tell you what: I'll let you keep these earrings for me.
We'll give them to her together after the party. How's that?

> *He gives her the earrings. Cille does not an-
> swer. Offstage, we hear Adelaide laugh.*

Listen to her. What's Adelaide up to these days?

CILLE

Dan.

CLARENCE

She doesn't want him.

CILLE

No. She wants you.

CLARENCE
Shrugs.

Not really.

CILLE

Not really, no. It's worse than if she really did.

CLARENCE

She's just a flirt.

CILLE

I don't think she's just a . . .
> Adelaide enters. Closes door. She wears a
> black frilly party dress with too much black
> lace, and carries a black fan.

ADELAIDE

Clarence, I'd like to speak to you.
> *To Cille.*

Alone.

CLARENCE
To Cille.

You can stay. Adelaide and I don't have any secrets.

ADELAIDE

That's right. Clarence keeps his secrets with other people.
We don't have any secrets.

CLARENCE

Well, what is it?

ADELAIDE

It's just that it's . . . been a long time since . . . since I've
been coming over here. If your mama's going to start inviting outsiders . . . I mean, it does seem to me somebody
ought to form a decision. And you being the man of the
house . . .

CLARENCE

What kind of decision do you have to form?

61

ADELAIDE

Oh no. I've already formed mine. I'm just waiting.

CLARENCE

Waiting for what?

ADELAIDE

The party concerned to make up his mind.

CLARENCE

Him? He'll grow up.

ADELAIDE
Softly.

Will he?

A pause. She smiles.

I sometimes wonder how anybody can grow up around here. With all the pretending.

CLARENCE

Don't *you* ever do any pretending?

ADELAIDE

A little. But I have to. Why else would your mama allow me in the house?

Titters.

I sometimes think she is the most alone woman I ever saw. She's even alone inside her own family. And you know what else I think, Clarence? It seems to me you're in a trap.

CLARENCE

It seems to me my life is none of your business.

ADELAIDE

Trapped animals are everybody's business.

Goes to window.

What a beautiful night.

Spreads her skirt.

My mama once sent me to ballet school for a year. Makes me feel like . . . dancing out there in the moonlight. Don't it make you feel like dancing, Clarence?

CLARENCE

No.

ADELAIDE
Begins to move slowly around them.
Did anyone ever see such a . . . carved moon?

CILLE
That's what they call a three-quarters moon.

ADELAIDE
Is that what they call it? Seems such a ordinary description. So much arithmetic.

CLARENCE
The moon is made of algebra, Adelaide.
As she dances past him.
Not cheese.

ADELAIDE
Now listen to him. The moon is made of algebra; what funny descriptions you-all have . . . here I always thought it was made of wishes and hopes and silver, and dreams . . . or is that the stars?

CLARENCE
No. That's just people.

ADELAIDE
People? Not little boys, anyway.
Moving around him.
Little *boys* are made out of *snips* and *snails* and *puppy-dog* tails.

CLARENCE
No, Adelaide. Those are the stars.

ADELAIDE
Now you are making *fun* with me, Clarence Morris.
Titters. Stops moving. Puts one finger on his chest.

CLARENCE
Seriously.
Adelaide, you are the last person in the world I would ever make fun with.

ADELAIDE

Am I?

Takes finger off. Laughing softly.

Am I now? Well I almost don't know how to answer that.
But I ain't really here. None of us is. We are all just pieces
of your mama's mind. And I'm getting tired of waiting. This
is the waitingest house I was ever in.

CLARENCE

If you don't like it here, Adelaide, why don't you get out?

ADELAIDE

Smiling.

I might one day.

*Dan enters. Adelaide immediately resumes
her coy attitude.*

Well, now, here comes my official affianced fiancé.

To Dan, as Clarence moves around the room.

My, your brother's edgy tonight. Not that I blame him. With
all these strangers milling around.

Clarence moves away.

Clarence, I just love the way you walk.

DAN

Mama compared him to a tiger cat this morning.

ADELAIDE

Did she? How fascinating. I always wondered: is a cat really
male or female? The way it moves, I mean. Or does that
just depend on who strokes it last? Remember when we
were little . . . and we used to play the shadow game . . .
here in this kitchen? When I'd turn the lamp on

She turns it on.

and we'd make funny shadows on the wall?

*All begin to make shadows against the wall
with their hands and bodies. They let go and
seem to become children again. Ad-libs of
"Look at me," "What's this?" etc. Adelaide
tries to hold Clarence's attention as the mood
of the scene rises.*

64

This was *Mama's* game.

ADELAIDE
Hard.
They all were.
They stop abruptly.
That's the dangerous thing about you people: you just can't seem to stop playing your mama's games.
Clarence begins to tap nervously on the table.
You ought to try the one I taught you . . . for a change. Remember?
Softly, keeping rhythm to his tapping.
If you're yellow, you're mellow; if you're brown, stick around; if you're black, stand back, stand back, stand back. . . . If you're yellow, you're mellow; if you're brown . . .
Clarence joins in; then Dan. Finally Cille. They all dance and chant together. Adelaide keeps close to Clarence. Celeste and Dewey enter, join in the dance. The fourth or fifth time around, on "If you're black . . ." Mama enters. The song stops.

MAMA
After a slight pause.
Stand back, stand back. The party's in there.

ADELAIDE
That's exactly what I've been trying to tell him. The party's in there.
All exit but Cille, who starts to go; remembers earrings, goes and gets them. Holds them up to the light, turns and runs out to yard. Dewey enters and follows her outside.

DEWEY
You okay?

CILLE
Yes.

DEWEY

You ran out of that kitchen like you was on fire.

CILLE

I like it better outside sometimes.

DEWEY

Do you mind if I sit with you a while?

CILLE

I don't mind.

DEWEY

My sister's been trying to get us out here all evening.
                    Laughs awkwardly.
I think she thinks we going to sit here and neck or something.
                    Laughs. There is a short pause.
I think necking is adolescent, don't you?

CILLE

I don't know. Dewey—

DEWEY

Yes?

CILLE

What would you do . . . if you found something that was . . . stolen?

DEWEY

Stolen?
                    Cille hands him earrings.
Look pretty ordinary to me. Garnets. Couldn't be rubies. But where did you get them?

CILLE

I can't tell you that.

DEWEY

From the devil's right-hand man? Well, you better get rid of them. Ain't no sense turning them over to the police. Not

66

people like us. They'd think we had something to do with it, see?

CILLE

I see.

DEWEY

So get rid of them. Bury them. Throw them out there in the weeds.

CILLE

Do you think getting rid of them might stop the thief?

DEWEY

Who knows? Stop him this time.

CILLE

Then go ahead.

DEWEY

Sure, okay.
            Shrugs.
You take one and I'll take one. You say, "I'm killing the devil's right-hand man." Here goes.
            He throws one earring into the cemetery.
            Laughs.
Go on.

CILLE

I'm killing the devil's right-hand man . . . here goes.
            She throws the other one, laughing.

KERES

            Enters from the cemetery.
What in the hell are you kids doing?

DEWEY

            Draws back.
Who are you?

KERES

I'm . . . looking for Clarence Morris.

DEWEY

He's inside, he's having a party. This here is his sister.

KERES

Yeah. Well, just tell your brother Mr. Keres was here. From the telegraph company. They need him to come to work tonight.

CILLE
Simply.
I don't think they need him there. I won't tell him that.

KERES

You know, little girl, you oughtn't to put your nose into what isn't none of your business . . . you might get it hurt. Now just tell your brother what I said. Tell him I'll be waiting.
Exits.

DEWEY
Whistles.
Who was he?

CILLE
The devil's right-hand man.

DEWEY
Who?

CILLE
The man in the game we were playing.

DEWEY

Honey, this one ain't playing. This one's serious. How come you talked to him that way? He sure looked angry.

CILLE
He looked scared.

DEWEY

Scared? That creepy man? You must be imagining things.

CILLE

Don't say that. It's what everybody says: I have fits and imagine things.

68

DEWEY

I never heard it.

CILLE

Looks at him.

Yes you did, Dewey.

DEWEY

Well, I . . . I never paid any attention. I mean, I *know* about your headaches. I ought to know. Been filling them prescriptions long enough.

Shrugs.

Being delicate is attractive in a girl.

CILLE

I'm not delicate.

DEWEY

Lots of girls get headaches.

CILLE

Not like mine.

DEWEY

Okay, okay, so what? So you got your own brand of head-ache. Say . . . what brings them on, anyway?

CILLE

Points directly at audience.

You see that graveyard there?

DEWEY

Certainly I see it. It's the same as the one back there.

CILLE

Our father is buried there. At night . . . sometimes I just come out here and sit. I like to watch the shells . . .

DEWEY

Squints at audience.

You referring to them white clamshells . . . in between the graves?

CILLE

Some nights they get so white . . . they hurt your eyes in the darkness. And sometimes . . . the white clamshell dust rises. Like heat waves. If you try to look . . . it makes you sick. Only the thing is . . . sometimes I *have* to look.

DEWEY

Have to why?

CILLE

Some nights I don't believe anything. When everything is a lie . . . everything in the whole world . . . except the dust. Then it happens. The trees move. The white light inside my head burns . . . and the pain comes. Then . . . I go blind. For a while.

DEWEY

Is that all?

CILLE

Yes.

DEWEY

Them famous sick spells? My Lord, I thought it was something serious. That just comes from overstraining the eyes. You got to wear glasses.

CILLE

Mama took me to an eye doctor.

DEWEY

And?

CILLE

He says . . . I have perfect vision.

DEWEY

Well then? What are you worried for? All you got to do is stop trying to see through things.

CILLE

I can't stop.

70

DEWEY

What you mean, you can't stop? I don't see at night. Look
at me.
Squints at audience.
I don't see a damn thing but a graveyard.

CILLE

They have a simple name for headaches like mine. They
call them migraine.

DEWEY

Do the pills help?

CILLE

Not much. Sometimes I stay blind for three hours. Does
that scare you?

DEWEY

Hell no. Why should it?

CILLE

It scares some people.

DEWEY

Like who?

CILLE

Mama.

DEWEY

Well I ain't your mama, and you don't perturb me one little
bit. Specially since you explained it to me. I doubt whether
I'd even call for help. I'd just sit right here and keep you
company till it was over.
Clears his throat. Gracefully.
Go ahead. Have a headache.

CILLE
Smiling.
Tonight is different. Even the wind feels different.

DEWEY

There ain't no wind at all.

71

CILLE

Yes, there is. I can feel it.
>*Gently.*

Dewey.

DEWEY

Yes.

CILLE

Kiss me.
>*Dewey leans forward awkwardly, kisses her.*

Did I do it right?

DEWEY

Course.
>*Clears his throat.*

Only . . . you shouldn't talk so soon . . . afterwards. I mean you shouldn't talk right away.
>*He kisses her again.*

CILLE

Like that?

DEWEY

Certainly, like that. You shouldn't always talk so soon. It ruins the mood.
>*There is another, longer kiss. Cille presses against him. Dewey pulls his head back. Hoarsely.*

Cille. Are you a virgin?

CILLE

>*Lets go; breaks away.*

You shouldn't always talk so soon.

DEWEY

I don't know much about virgins. I mean, who is and who ain't. I get confused. Take my sister, for instance. She goes with a boy named Eddie Rhodes. So I asked her once. I said, "Sister, are you a virgin?"
>*A pause.*

She said, "I wasn't up until I met Eddie, but I am now."

> *They kiss again as Celeste enters from the living room and crosses to the gallery.*

CELESTE

Where are they? Must be outside.

> *She goes out. Adelaide and Dan are behind her. To Cille.*

Your mama's going to get us with the Bible. She wants us to read . . . Oh, for heaven's sake . . .

> *Embarrassed at having interrupted them.*

Honey, the thing is she wants Dewey and me to read the Bible to her. Can you imagine? Of all the times to pick . . .

ADELAIDE

> *Coming outside, followed by Dan.*

It's an old family custom, Miss Chipley. Daniel, would you mind telling your brother Clarence . . . I want *him* to bring me my purse? I believe I left my fan in it.

CELESTE

No, you didn't, honey. It's up your sleeve.

ADELAIDE

Oh, so it is. Yes, thank you. So it is.

CELESTE

You been on my tail all evening. Anybody would think . . .

ADELAIDE

> *Trying to drown her out.*

When I first heard it was a custom here for each visitor to read his favorite part of the Bible out loud . . . I said to Mrs. Morris, I said, "I'm awfully glad I'm not the mailman."

> *She breaks into high peals of laughter, followed by Dan. Celeste remains deadpan.*

DAN

> *To Celeste.*

Get it? Adelaide's glad she's not the mailman.

I am too.

ADELAIDE

Miss Chipley. Don't you think it's time now . . . for one of us to be sensible?

CELESTE

Which one?

ADELAIDE

I'm sure you have been glad to meet the Morris family, with all the loose gossip going around about them. But now that you have satisfied your curiosity . . . there are more problems here than meet the eye. Do I make my meaning clear?

CELESTE

Keep going.

ADELAIDE

Why don't you leave this house for the people who are accustomed to it?

CELESTE

Why don't you run your ass up North and get it Simonized?

ADELAIDE

Rises. After a pause.

Well, precious. Maybe we'll see who is welcome here.

Runs into kitchen.

Mrs. Morris . . .

Exits into living room.

DAN

To Celeste.

You shouldn't ever treat Adelaide like that. *You shouldn't.*

Follows Adelaide into the house.

CELESTE

To Cille, putting on her lipstick.

Sorry, honey, I couldn't help it. I was okay till she started burping all through the ambrosia, with that stomach trouble.

74

First her mama got the Virulent Diabetes and told everybody she was going to die. And did. Now Adelaide acts just
like she's going to die too. I just hate people who are always
boasting. She ain't got no pain of any kind. Not in her stomach, anyway. You know what that is, that ache, like a cramp,
she gets right over here?

> MAMA
> *Calling from living room.*

Where is she?

> CELESTE

A constipated heart.

> MAMA
> *Enters kitchen going outside.*

Is she all right? Where is my daughter?

> CELESTE

She's right out there, Mrs. Morris.
> *She goes into living room.*

> MAMA

Out there? What are you two doing?
> *To Dewey as he comes into kitchen with Cille.*

Lucille ain't like one of these girls you take out from around
here.
> *Clarence enters.*

My daughter is special. She gets . . . weak spells.

> DEWEY

Yes, ma'am, she told me.

> MAMA

She . . . told you. She . . .
> *To Clarence.*

told him . . .

> CLARENCE

It's all right, Mama.

DEWEY

We was just coming inside to read the Bible to you, Mrs.
Morris . . . We was just coming in . . .
> *Exits to living room.*

ADELAIDE
> *Enters from living room with Dan.*

And *I* was just leaving. Good night, Clarence.

MAMA

But . . . don't you care for some more ambrosia and . . .

ADELAIDE

No indeed: I have already partaken of an ample sufficiency.
My condition seems to be getting more and more delicate.
And I don't think I have even been paid a compliment on
my party dress.
> *To Clarence.*

Well?

CLARENCE

I don't like black dresses.

ADELAIDE
> *Softly.*

Why, you never told me that. That's the last humiliation.

MAMA

Daniel does.

DAN

I do. I think you look like a . . . a plastic kewpie doll. In
mourning.

ADELAIDE

Thank you.
> *To Clarence.*

But I think the weather and the company around here is
getting too warm for kewpie dolls, don't you? There was a
second this evening I was afraid I might just melt down to
my real self.

76

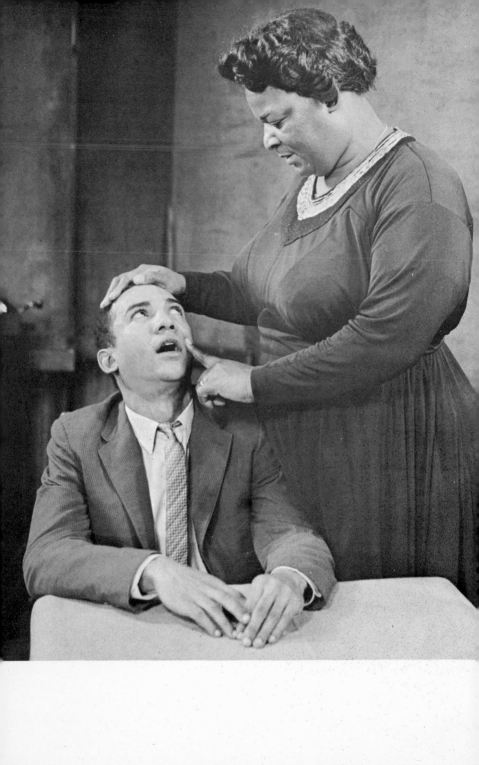

CLARENCE

Do you have a real self, Adelaide?

ADELAIDE

After a pause.

You stick around, sugar. You might see.

She exits with Dan. Mama follows to the gallery.

CLARENCE

To Cille.

That is practically a walking definition of a bitch.

MAMA

Going back into kitchen.

I think them neighbors must of said something to upset her.

CILLE

It wasn't just the neighbors.

MAMA

Frowns. To Cille.

Are you feeling well?

CILLE

Yes, Mama.

She exits.

CLARENCE

That boy didn't hurt her, Mama. She's all right.

MAMA

She worries me. You don't know the things she imagines in her head. This morning she said that you . . .

With difficulty.

wanted to leave here. Right now. Even before you get your draft notice.

CLARENCE

Did she?

MAMA

Course I told her: with only three more payments on the

77

house. And everything. I explained to her you wouldn't go off and . . .

CLARENCE
Dully.
You don't have to worry about the payments, Mama.
Violently.
Stop worrying about money.

SITTRE
Opening living-room door.
Book of Job, Sister Nora.

MAMA
Thank you, Deacon.
As she exits.
My son always did know how to take care of things.
Clarence goes outside and calls.

CLARENCE
Keres . . . Keres . . .
Keres enters.
Where the hell have you been?

KERES
Waiting for you. I been perched out on that tombstone a half hour. That crazy sister of yours wouldn't tell you I was here. She was outside throwing cheap jewelry into the graveyard.
Hands earring to him.
I dug one of them out of the weeds.

CLARENCE
What the hell is she up to?

KERES
Who knows? I'd watch out for her if I was you.

CLARENCE
Keres . . . I need three thousand dollars.

KERES
In a whisper.

You what? Three thousand . . . What's wrong with you? Say, has your uncle been after you again?

CLARENCE
Softly; viciously.
I want enough to pay him off for good. I want enough to line this house in silver. Before I leave.

KERES
Are you crackers or something?

CLARENCE
No.

KERES
Then why . . .

CLARENCE
I'm going to be drafted soon.

KERES
Drafted or not. There ain't a way in the world you can make that much. Not with your finicky ways. You break into one empty house . . . once a month. You've got to open up the gates, Clarence, if you want to make real money. By the way . . . Mrs. Soren wants to see you tonight. She said to tell you the painting's not finished.

CLARENCE
I'm not going back there.

KERES
Clarence, if you go on all fours you're going. This woman is one of my best clients. She is married to the vice-president of the telegraph company.

CLARENCE
I don't work for . . .

KERES
So what? You used to. That's how she saw you. Come to think of it that's how I first saw you too . . . just a kid riding

79

out on a bicycle to deliver telegrams to people. I said to you right then, I said, "Sonny, with looks like yours . . ."

CLARENCE

I remember what you said. Just don't ever tell me what to do. You're only a second-rate fence for stolen goods. And a pimp.

KERES

Second-rate, hell. I'm a fence, a pimp, a narcotics vendor, an agent for artists' models, a bird watcher and a general Handy Man. At least I know what I am. Which is more than I can say for you. Even when she sent for you to pose, that's all you did. The first ten times. Just pose.
Looking at him.
How much did she give you the last time?

CLARENCE

A hundred dollars.

KERES

I'm a son of a bitch, that dirty old lady. Well, congratulations.

CLARENCE

I'm not that kind of man, Keres. That's just one thing I'm not.

KERES

One thing? I'm so sick of hearing what you're not, I've got it coming out of my ears. "I'm not a criminal. I'm not a hustler, sometimes I'm not even a thief. I'm not, I'm not, I'm not." *What are you, Clarence?*

CLARENCE

Shut up.

KERES

I'll shut up. But if you think I can raise three thousand dollars just getting rid of cheap silver candlesticks and lousy gold rings for you, you think again. You've got to be willing

to do anything you have to for that kind of money. You understand me? *Anything.*
> *He starts out.*

CLARENCE
Flat.
Go tell her I'll be there tonight.

KERES
That's a little bit better.

CLARENCE
Going up to gallery.
Tonight and tomorrow night. And any night after that. Find out who's in town and who can pay.

KERES
Comes back. A pause.
What did you say? You mean . . . even . . .

CLARENCE
I mean anybody. Make all the contacts you can, and fast.
> *A pause.*
Well, what are you waiting for? *Get going.*

KERES
I never could figure out what makes you tick. But I always did admire you, Clarence. Always. You know what you just did? You just grew up. Right in front of my eyes.
> *Grins and reaches up to Clarence's shoulder.*
I'll tell her. We're finally on our way, friend.
> *Whispers.*
Yes indeed. We're on our way . . .
> *He exits.*

> *Clarence goes into the house, starts into his room, as Cille enters.*

CILLE
He was here again, wasn't he?

CLARENCE
*Stops. They are now standing in the same po-
sitions as at the beginning of the play.*

Who?

CILLE

The man who says he's from the telegraph company.

CLARENCE

Sister, leave me alone. I'm warning you.
He goes out to yard. Tangles in clotheslines.
Goddam her clotheslines. She'll kill us with them one day.
Not that she'd mind if we were dead.

CILLE
Follows him.
Mama only wants us to be safe. Not dead.

CLARENCE

Mama doesn't know the difference. Will you for heaven's
sake stop staring at me?

CILLE
Follows to gallery.
Once before you had that look on your face. I was standing
on the gallery when you got off your bicycle. I was here, and
. . . you had the telegram in a yellow envelope, and your
uniform on; only . . . at first I could hardly see you; because
of the light. And you leaned the bicycle against the cemetery wall. There, where the sun was setting in the center
of all the brightness. You came walking straight out of the
sun. With that same dead face.

CLARENCE
Taut.
If you imagine things in your brain you'll have bad dreams
at night.

CILLE
Softly.
My dreams are only bad when I'm awake.

82

CLARENCE

Then you see things that aren't there.

CILLE

Stop it, Clarence.

CLARENCE

Stop it? Stop it, stop it, stop it, Clarence.
Harshly.
My God. I wake up to Mama's record, and sleep in her
house, and I walk. While you stand around on the gallery,
and . . . watch.

CILLE

Go away from here, Clarence.

CLARENCE

I can't go. Not unless I . . .
He stops.

CILLE

Not unless you tell Mama about the telegram?

CLARENCE

*Backs her look a second. Then turns slightly
away.*
What do you mean by that?

CILLE

I don't ever mean anything but what I say.

CLARENCE

Forget it.
He turns again and looks at her.
Tell her what, for Christ sake?

CILLE

Simply; gently.
You can just say it was a present for her to feel better. Tell
her how you made it, and brought it home to give to her.
Tell her that George is still alive.

83

CLARENCE

You think I made that telegram . . . you think . . . I would tell Mama that George is dead . . . to make her *feel better?*

CILLE

If that *was* why you did it, tell her so.

CLARENCE

A phony telegram? Take a chance like that?

CILLE

You would of taken any chance. You knew, ever since George ran off and left us, that the only thing Mama wanted to hear was that he was dead.

CLARENCE

You're crazy.

CILLE

Is that what Uncle Sittre knows about: the telegram? Is that how he makes you pay? . . . Clarence. You got to tell the truth now.

CLARENCE

You and your crazy truth. How do you think the truth would fit in that house?

CILLE

Where is George?

CLARENCE

Where *is* he? Where do you think he is?

CILLE

I remember him, Clarence. He never would have gone in the army.

CLARENCE

Why wouldn't he?

CILLE

Because he was a coward. He was worse than that. Mama was scared she might have turned him into a criminal or

84

worse . . . Is that what happened? The way he left he could have done anything. Did he kill somebody?

CLARENCE
Backing away from her.
Leave me alone. Some nights you got eyes like . . .

CILLE
My eyes are the same as Mama's. It's the only way we look alike. Clarence, where is he, in jail?

CLARENCE
Recoiling from her. Whispers.
What the hell power on earth makes you know things?

CILLE
I never did learn how not to know.

CLARENCE
How long . . . have you been thinking that telegram wasn't real?

CILLE
I knew it wasn't real when you brought it home.

CLARENCE
Pointing at her.
Now listen: you're wrong.

CILLE
No, I ain't.

CLARENCE
Ain't?
Harshly; brokenly.
Who taught you to say ain't? Say *isn't*. You can say *am not*. You know better than that, for God's sake. I taught you myself. Don't say ain't.

CILLE
I'm not wrong.

85

CLARENCE

All right. Supposing . . . Just . . . supposing you were right.
Suppose he never went into the army. Suppose . . . George
went up North, and went wild, and did something. . . .
And they caught him and put him in jail for a long, long
time. Longer even than Mama is going to live. Supposing
that was true . . . should I tell her that?

CILLE

Yes.

CLARENCE

And if you know so much . . . then maybe you know . . .
it would kill her now to hear a thing like that. The same as
it would have killed her then.

CILLE

I don't think it would. But even if it did . . . you got to tell
her, Clarence.

CLARENCE

Staring at her.

You . . . knew all along . . . and you never said . . .

CILLE

You wouldn't let me talk about it. Nobody would. Besides,
you can lie so easily. I didn't think you cared.

CLARENCE

As though he had been slapped.

My God. My God, you didn't think I cared? You knew about
it, and . . .

Laughs.

You didn't think . . . I quit my job that day, don't you know
that? Didn't you wonder why I never went back there
again? Why I couldn't even walk into the telegraph office
without wanting to . . .

He faces her. Accusingly.

How do you imagine I learned to make a telegram like that?
I was young once too, you know. Once, once, once I was
young.

86

He turns away; moves to the house.

Mama wouldn't even eat when he left. She wouldn't talk. I watched her throat working . . . trying to swallow the pain. But she couldn't. She just sat in that chair, and looked . . . and I never saw anybody hurt so much.

Shouts.

She couldn't even ask for help, except with her face. There wasn't anybody to help her but me. Don't you understand? It was the only thing I knew how to do: it was the only way I could help her.

He reaches up for the clotheslines. Helplessly.

How do you imagine I learned to make a telegram like that? You didn't know I had delivered real telegrams too . . . *real* telegrams to mothers whose sons were really dead? I wish you would have had to see their faces. Every day. To stand and watch their faces. And listen to them scream. Most of them did, you know. They just stood still and screamed. You really think I could have gone back to delivering telegrams . . . like that . . . after what I did? You didn't think I cared? *You didn't think . . .*

He puts a fist against his mouth and turns away.

CILLE

Mama didn't scream. She only smiled.

CLARENCE

That's right. That's what Mama did. Mama smiled. And right then I could hear the voices of those other women . . . all at the same time. I watched her smile. And I could hear them scream.

CILLE

Moving toward him.

Go in and tell her, Clarence.

CLARENCE

Keep away from me. Keep away. And remember this: don't ever trust me.

He faces the gallery.

I belong to her. As much as that telegram does, and this house. As much as her biggest dreams. Because I am the biggest dream of all. I am Mama's most important pretend.

CILLE

Is that what you want to be?

CLARENCE

Want to be? It doesn't matter what I want. It never did.

CILLE

Clarence, you feel sorrier for yourself than anybody I ever met.

CLARENCE

You never met anybody.

CILLE

I think you are a coward.

CLARENCE

Sister, I warned you . . .

CILLE

You warned me, yes. I'm not scared of you, Clarence. You even lie to yourself. You want to pretend you're doing it all for Mama. Well, you're not. Not any more. That's what's happened to you, isn't it? It's you who would die if she found out.
Hard.
You're not protecting Mama any more. *You're only protecting yourself.*
Clarence raises his arm to strike her.
Go ahead.
A pause. She turns and goes into house.

CLARENCE

Where are you going?
He follows her.

CILLE

To do it for you.

88

CLARENCE

Do what?

CILLE

Tell her about the telegram: I will tell her it's not real.

CLARENCE
Whispers.

What is it?

CILLE

A piece of paper in a frame. That's all.

CLARENCE

Is it?
Fiercely.
It's got her whole heart in it. Do you think you can walk past that?
As if in answer, Cille passes the telegram.
I love her, Cille.

CILLE

I love her too.
She calls.
Mama.

CLARENCE

Don't you remember how you got your first headache? It was when Mama made you watch the telegram and pray. It wasn't the white dust, not the first time.
Carefully.
It was watching the telegram.

CILLE
Staring at it.
Clarence, don't you . . . try to make me . . .

CLARENCE

I think you'd better clean the air, you're blinking.

CILLE

I'm not.

Makes the movement with her hands.

The wind just stopped . . .

CLARENCE

There was no wind. Look at it.

CILLE

Clarence . . .

CLARENCE

You wouldn't think a thing like that can make you sick. Look, look, look, look, look at it.

> *There is a pause. Clarence turns his back on her; goes into his room.*

> *Mama enters kitchen.*

MAMA

Did you call?

> *A pause.*

Well? What are you staring at that for?

CILLE

It's not . . .

MAMA

Not what?

CILLE

> *Calls loud.*

Real.

MAMA

Let me feel your head . . .

CILLE

No. Let me go . . .

> *Breaks away from her. Runs out to gallery.*

MAMA

Come back here.

> *Calls.*

Deacon Sittre.

90

CILLE

Clarence . . . please . . . where are you?
She gropes her way forward.

Deacon Sittre comes into kitchen.

MAMA

Help me with her: it looks bad this time.

CILLE

Clarence . . . Please . . .
*Cille falls down the steps as Mama and Dea-
con Sittre rush out to her. She stands up, tears
away from them. She rushes blindly forward,
collides with tree.*

Beating the tree with her fists, yells in rage.
I hate this house. It's all a lie. It's a lie. I don't believe it.
Please, Clarence . . .
*Deacon Sittre takes her away from tree.
Dewey and Celeste run out to yard in time to
see Cille strike out at Deacon Sittre.*

MAMA

I have her now.
*Holds Cille, who is sobbing. To Dewey and
Celeste.*
My daughter is sick. Please. I ask you. Don't stare at us. Get
out.
Dewey and Celeste exit quickly left.

SITTRE

I'd better be getting home myself. It's late.
Exits up right.

MAMA

To Cille, holding her in her lap.
Clarence left my baby all alone. Hush, honey, hush. Mama
will take care of everything.
Looks up.
Is that old cloud still up there? Hush.

91

Tensely; hard.

That cloud will get off my house if I have to make it rain personally. Yes indeed.

Cille's sobs die away. Behind Mama, Clarence has slipped silently out of his bedroom window. He stands watching her for a second, then runs up and exits into the cemetery.

Mama shakes her fist at the sky. She repeats.

If I have to make it rain.

She yells suddenly.

If I have to make it rain . . .

CURTAIN

Act Two

Three weeks later. Eight a.m. on a Sunday morning.

After Curtain, eight chimes of the church bell. Hard gray light outside, shining through thick clouds which are building to rain. The stage is empty. The pipe-lamp is on over the telegram.

Mama's house is not quite the same as before. Dark yellow curtains over both windows and a bright new stove undermine the feeling of stark poverty. The shadows are thicker. The telegram has been transferred to a wide silver frame; a triangular blood-red cloth hangs from the shelf below. All of the additions seem a little out of place in their surroundings. The house looks softer almost against its own will.

Mama enters from the living room, closing the door behind her. She wears a plain but obviously expensive black silk dress with a silver-beaded collar. Humming to herself, she lights stove burner under coffeepot; looks out window. Goes out screen door, down steps, glances at sky. Nods knowingly. Takes four shirts in off clothesline. Re-enters house, drops them in basket. Starts to wind clock. Stops. Looks stealthily at Clarence's door. Turns on overhead light. Takes letter from pocket of her dress; unfolds it; tries to decipher it; cannot. Folds and replaces it carefully in her pocket.

Takes out phonograph, winds it, puts record on—as Clarence enters softly behind her from his bedroom. He is in black trousers and a long-sleeved shirt, a towel around his neck. Mama plays the record. It has barely begun when it catches on the word "God." The single word continues to repeat. Finally Mama goes over; lifts needle off slowly, peers at record, holding it between her hands. Behind her, Clarence goes to the door, waits—then slams it hard and loud. Mama jumps; fumbles the record; catches it; at the last moment she loses her balance and breaks it herself on the sideboard. Clarence stands watching her, trying to keep a straight face. Mama turns slowly and stares at him. A long pause. Then she turns back to the sideboard, flips it open, and takes out a brand-new copy of the record. Holds it high.

CLARENCE
As if she were pointing a gun at him.
I give up.

MAMA
Good thing I saved up this extra copy for the emergencies without telling nobody about it. Mr. Newcomb at the record store is after getting me my new one from New York City. He says . . .

CLARENCE
Mr. Newcomb says anything he can think of to get you out of his shop. There aren't any more copies of that record.

MAMA
Who told you that?

CLARENCE
Mr. Newcomb did.

94

MAMA

That's a lie.

CLARENCE

All right, Mama, it's a lie. I wonder how you'll wake us up when the last copy breaks.

MAMA

You don't have a very good memory.

CLARENCE

Of what?

Stretches.

MAMA

Of me. And you. In that chair. Before there was no record.
She hums to him. Clarence suddenly throws arms around her and holds her.
All right now: that's enough of that.

CLARENCE

Ashamed of his display of emotion. Crosses to doorway.
Is that Dan in the bathroom?
Calls.
You coming out this year?

MAMA

Leave him alone, he just went in.
Puts record and phonograph back in sideboard.
I am putting my record away for one reason, and one reason alone. I want to talk to you.

CLARENCE

Oh my God.

MAMA

Don't you swear.

CLARENCE

That's not swearing, Mama. It's praying.

MAMA

It is taking the Lord's name in vain. I'll get your coffee.

CLARENCE

Sighs resignedly. Sits.

What happened to Cille?

MAMA

Getting coffee.

Ain't nothing happened to her. We run out of milk. I sent her over to the dairy truck.

CLARENCE

At seven o'clock in the morning?

MAMA

Me and your sister gets up at six. Anyhow, it's going to rain later on. I never saw such a hurricane sky. Had to turn the light on.

CLARENCE

The dairy truck. First time you've allowed her that far out of the house in three weeks. You've been so scared she'd get another . . .

MAMA

That was the worst seizure she ever had. I don't want her getting another one no time soon. Anyway, she ain't going to have no trouble on an empty stomach.

CLARENCE

You sent her out without any breakfast?

MAMA

How about if you pays a little less attention to me and a little bit more to yourself?

Gives him his coffee.

Slipping around like a shadow all over my house. Only person I ever knew could step on a creaky board without making it sound. All my life I saw you before I heard you; but just lately it's been too much. Now I don't even see you first. I see your shadow.

96

CLARENCE

Sipping coffee. Boredly.

Up to yesterday I was a tiger cat.

MAMA

Angrily.

Today you're a shadow. Puts me all on edge.

CLARENCE

Maybe I'm fading.

MAMA

You ain't faded none.

> *Grabs his shoulder, pushes it, making him spill coffee. Lets him go. Definitively.*

You ain't faded none.

CLARENCE

Okay, Mama. I'll try walking on the other side of the light. Is that what you wanted to talk about?

MAMA

No, it ain't. And you knows it ain't.

> *Sits facing him.*

Clarence, I want to know how come you are still saving that printed letter.

CLARENCE

> *Puts cup down. Stares at her. A slight pause. He rises slowly.*

Have you been going through the suitcase under my bed?

> *Dan opens the living-room door; he is washed and half dressed.*

MAMA

Good morning, lamb. Go ahead and get yourself all dressed.

> *He goes back into the living room.*

And shut the door: I'm a lady.

> *Dan shuts the living-room door.*

I am talking about the letter you got last Monday . . . when you told me the sweepstakes company sent you a six-hundred-dollar prize. Only you never showed it to nobody else but me. And last night when I was dusting . . .

CLARENCE

Give it to me, Mama.

MAMA
Hands letter to him, open.
I just don't understand how come it's back here, when you said you cashed it in. Besides. There is something familiar to me about them words at the top of that page.

CLARENCE

You don't even know your own name in print. How could you recognize a word?

MAMA

That's what's so funny. I did.

CLARENCE
Folds letter; puts it in pocket of jacket.
You had no right to take anything out of my suitcase.

MAMA

Now don't you use that tone to me. I didn't even notice what else was there.

CLARENCE

Didn't you, Mama?

MAMA

I just passed over everything with a dust rag like I always do. There wasn't nothing in there but that new life insurance policy you got for yourself the other day and the letter.

CLARENCE

And where was the letter?

MAMA

It was under the insurance policy . . . Well, I had to dust the underside too.

CLARENCE

I should have known better than to trust you.

MAMA

I just got to wondering, that's all. And I never did see so much stuff as you brought home lately. New sofa and a chair in the living room; the material for them new curtains. The velvet, and the stove. And when you made the three last payments on this house . . . all three payments at once . . .

CLARENCE

Are you complaining?

MAMA

No, I ain't. Ain't exactly complaining. I just don't like having too many expensive things around. Gives folks the wrong impression.

CLARENCE

Seems to me you are forgetting one expensive thing.

MAMA

No sir. I didn't forget it. The frame is different.

CLARENCE

Why?

MAMA

Because we went downtown and bought it together. The only one they had with a guarantee.
Crosses to telegram. Softly. Proudly.
A Guaranteed Permanent Frame.
Turns to him. With a certain shyness.
You didn't even notice. I'm wearing my new dress.

CLARENCE

I noticed.
Cille enters yard left with milk bottles.

MAMA

Plain can't wait for Adelaide to see me in it. She was here last night, did I tell you?

CLARENCE

She's here every night.

99

MAMA

And today we going to meet her at church and . . . But that ain't what I'm talking about. You can always make me change the subject. I was talking about that letter . . .

CLARENCE

To Cille as she comes into kitchen.

Good morning.

A pause.

I *said,* good morning.

Cille doesn't answer. Clarence exits into living room.

MAMA

What took you so long?

CILLE

I had to walk to Dauphine.

MAMA

All the way to Dauphine?

CILLE

The truck doesn't stop here on Sundays, Mama.

MAMA

I forgot.

Going for milk. Automatically.

Did you talk to anybody?

CILLE

Only the milkman.

MAMA

The milkman talked to you?

CILLE

No, Mama. I talked to him.

MAMA

He better not get fresh with you.

100

CILLE

He won't, Mama. People don't. Did everybody have coffee?

MAMA

Daniel ain't yet; he's in putting on his new clothes. How come you won't even wear your brand new dress and your wrist watch that Clarence bought for you? You could wear them things today. Today is Sunday.

CILLE

This dress is fine.

MAMA

That old rag? You are a mystery to me. First thing I remember your saying no to me about in your whole life. Don't you want to look pretty?

CILLE

I'm not pretty, Mama. And I like this dress.

MAMA

No wonder that Dewey Chipley don't want to be left alone with you, even in broad daylight.

CILLE

That's not why.

MAMA

Takes out bowl.

Not that I blame him exactly. After you going blind like that, his first night. Right in his face. His sister said it scared him so bad they had to give him paregoric. He ain't such a bad boy, though. Come calling every Saturday morning for three weeks.

CILLE

He didn't come yesterday.

MAMA

With that sad face. And that little bunch of sticky flowers.

CILLE

It was you told him to keep bringing flowers, Mama.

MAMA

For my telegram, not for no hospital. I hope he keeps on bringing them, too, wilted or not. I can always fix them up nice. I just wish he wouldn't walk in here like he thought it was a sick ward or something.

Imitates mournful expression.

"Good morning, Lucille." With them sticky little cornflowers. Daniel, you want some grits?

DAN

Enters, dressed in a new suit.

No, ma'am.

MAMA

Don't have to say ma'am less you want to. Mama will do. "No thank you, Mama."

DAN

No thank you, Mama.

MAMA

Why not?

DAN

I just don't want any.

MAMA

Ought to put something solid inside your stomach. I don't like the way you been looking lately. Peakèd. Kind of naked around the eyes. Don't appear like you slept in weeks.

DAN

I feel okay.

CLARENCE

Entering.

He's not sick, Mama. He even took a bath. He's in love, remember?

MAMA

Is that it?

102

CLARENCE

He's never even kissed a girl; have you?

MAMA

Adelaide kissed him on the cheek last night.

CLARENCE

Did he faint?

MAMA

He did not. He just been carrying on like a man who's
going to be married.
To Dan. Giving him coffee.
Well, we going to see her right now. You told her it was your
turn to take me to church, didn't you?
To Clarence.
Adelaide told Daniel most likely she would have a *an-
nouncement* to make today. To him and me.

CLARENCE

That's all I need this morning. Adelaide.

DAN
Suddenly. Deep.
You shut up.

CLARENCE
Stops.
What was that?

DAN

Shut up. Just keep your mouth off her whole name. She
ain't yours to talk about. Adelaide belongs to me.

CLARENCE
To Mama.
Congratulations. You actually made it happen, didn't you?
He holds Mama's arm up, like a prize fighter.
Announces.
The winner.
Exits into his room.

MAMA
To Dan.
Never mind what he says, lamb. She does belong to you.
Gives him coffee; pats his head, sighs.
My lamb. I got one son is my shadow and one is my lamb.

CLARENCE
Entering.
And one on the wall.

MAMA
That's enough.
Cille exits.
Don't always answer me back in front of the children. Who do you think I am?

CLARENCE
According to the United States Government you're a dependent.

MAMA
I'm a *what?*

CLARENCE
That's what *I* said.

MAMA
You want some grits before we go?

CLARENCE
No.

MAMA
No, what?

CLARENCE
Sits against the table. Boredly.
Just no.

MAMA
Are you looking for trouble today? You going to get it that way.

CLARENCE

I'm going to get it any way.

MAMA

And don't sit up on the edge of the table like that. Mr. Shadow Man. You are always sitting on the edge of things.

SITTRE

Entering at Riverview gates.

Everybody ready?

MAMA

Calls.

Hello, Deacon Sittre. We're coming right away.

SITTRE

Better hurry. We might have a little rain.

MAMA

I don't believe I ever knew a sky to look so dirty all over.

SITTRE

That is heaven, Sister Nora.

MAMA

Heaven looks like it needs a good laundress.

DAN

Let's go, Mama.

MAMA

I can feel the wet right around my fingers: we better take the umbrella.

DAN

I'll get it.

Exits to living room. Sittre comes into kitchen.

MAMA

Sighs. To Sittre.

It's thoughtful of you to come and take us to church, Deacon: since we started going separate. I plain can't get used to having that many valuables in the house which it would matter if somebody broke in or not.

SITTRE

You better get used to valuables, Sister Nora. Something tells me there's a lot more like them on the way.

MAMA

I don't see how there could be too many more. Besides, we got locks on all the closets now. What could anybody steal?

SITTRE

Now your Guaranteed Permanent Frame doesn't have a lock. And it's pure silver.

MAMA

Ain't a man born of woman would dare touch that telegram. Not even a thief.

SITTRE
Watching Mama and Clarence.
Not even a thief. That's a funny thing to say.

MAMA

It's true.

SITTRE
After a slight pause.
Yes. It is. Speaking of thieves, there was a little bit of a ruckus over on Decatur Street night before last, I understand.

MAMA

Decatur Street? That ain't too far from here. Maybe that's what I heard.

SITTRE

It seems this man had been taking presents and . . . other things from a rich married lady . . . name of Mrs. Soren.

MAMA

Soren? Why, I know her. Ain't she . . .

SITTRE

They call her the wife of the telegraph company.

MAMA

That's the one. Clarence knows her too.

SITTRE

I thought he might. It seems her husband and two of her sons got mind of a . . . relationship she was having that was considered . . . unfitting.
Smiles.
The man in question was colored. He was a thief.

MAMA

No.

CLARENCE

No.

SITTRE

Yes.
Smiles.
The men found out in time. They caught the thief out on the gallery of her house, handing over some jewelry to his fence.

MAMA

Fence?

SITTRE

Agent, Sister Nora.

CLARENCE

Agent.

SITTRE

They caught him . . . and they beat him all over his body with a big sack of firewood . . .

MAMA

Good for them.

SITTRE

I believe they did it that way in order not to kill the man

107

and cause a scandal. But they marked him up quite badly, they said . . . before he got away.

MAMA
Interested despite herself.
He got away?

SITTRE
Or else they let him go. On account of the lady's reputation, you understand. Mrs. Soren and her family have left town.

MAMA
I don't understand. Did the thief get the jewelry?

SITTRE
No. But they say he got away with almost . . . six hundred dollars. In cash.

MAMA
Six hundred . . .
Frowns. Shakes her head.
I don't know what the world is coming to. A thief like that wandering around loose . . .

SITTRE
Not just a ordinary thief either: this young man . . . is what they call a hustling thief.

CLARENCE
You're going to miss the service.
Goes to door and calls.
Dan.

SITTRE
Smiles.
Or a thieving hustler.

MAMA
Hustler?

SITTRE
That is vernacular, Sister Nora.

108

MAMA

Vernacular?

SITTRE

I'm afraid hustler is a vulgar term for a kind of . . . well . . .
Lowers his voice to a whisper.
male prostitute.

MAMA
Shocked.
Deacon Sittre Morris. On a Sunday. With the Reverend's
sermon right in your hand.

SITTRE

I beg your pardon, Sister Nora. I forget how deeply sensitive
you are.

MAMA

We'll just forget you said it, won't we, Clarence?

CLARENCE

Yes, Mama.

MAMA

It's time we got going.
Calls.
Daniel.

DAN
Off. Calls.
I can't find the umbrella, Mama.

MAMA

I'm coming.
To Clarence.
You'd best go back and wash your neck again. I thought I
saw a spot . . . I'll dash some water on my face, too.
Exits.

CLARENCE
Slowly.
God damn you.

SITTRE

I just wanted to make sure who the mysterious hustler was. Six hundred dollars is a great deal of money.

Clarence hands him an envelope full of money.

Let's see. Half of six is . . .

CLARENCE

You needn't count it. It's a thousand dollars.

SITTRE

A *thousand* . . .

CLARENCE

And it's all you're going to get from me. I just got my draft notice.

SITTRE

I thought that's what that letter was. Sweepstakes. Clarence, you do think of the cutest things.

CLARENCE

I didn't know if I could raise this much in time.

SITTRE

In time? In time for what?

Slowly.

For you to pay me off for good so I'd keep my mouth shut even while you're in the army.

Carefully.

But a thousand dollars is not enough for that.

CLARENCE

What? Why you dirty . . .

DAN

Entering.

I'll look in Clarence's room, Mama.

Exits.

CLARENCE

I could kill you.

SITTRE

You could. But you won't. You're not the type.

CLARENCE

Are you so damn sure of that?

SITTRE

Absolutely sure. Killing goes against your grain. I know a
killer when I see one. Your brother George, for instance.
He wouldn't ever have let me put the squeeze on him this
long.
    Smiles.
By the way, I have a piece of advice for you.

CLARENCE

I don't need . . .

SITTRE

You do need. You always need. You never learn. I'm afraid
Miss Adelaide could bring the whole house of cards tum-
bling down.

MAMA
    Entering with umbrella.
I got it, Daniel. Ready now, Deacon Sittre?
    Dan enters.

SITTRE

Off we go.

MAMA

You don't have to bring us home today. Daniel and me have
a private appointment after service. A certain party has a
announcement to make to us.

SITTRE

Really?
    Looking at Clarence.
A certain party?

MAMA

Tell Deacon Sittre how you feel about Adelaide.

111

I think she has a garden of glass that grows inside of her. She is delicate . . . I take care of Adelaide. I do.

SITTRE

Ain't that cute, huh? What a man.
As they go, calls back.
Better lock up, Clarence. There's no telling what the storm might bring in.
Slapping Dan on shoulder.
An announcement, huh?
Dan laughs happily.
An announcement . . .
They go out the gates.

A short pause. Cille enters; she picks up a stack of ironed clothes and starts for living room.

CLARENCE
Stops her. She looks at him.
When are you going to start speaking to me?

CILLE

I speak to you.

CLARENCE

Not unless you have to.
She doesn't answer.
Do you love me?

CILLE

Yes.

CLARENCE

Do you like me?

CILLE

No.

CLARENCE

Tell me . . . do you think things might be better if I wasn't here?

CILLE

I don't know.

CLARENCE

I asked you what you thought.

CILLE

I don't think any more, Clarence.
Flat.
I just do my work.

CLARENCE

It's hard to believe anything could make you give up the fight.

CILLE

Is it?

CLARENCE

Well, at least you've stopped worrying.

CILLE

Involuntarily.
I haven't; I'm worried about Dan.

CLARENCE

Dan? What's wrong with him?

CILLE

I think maybe he will need money very soon.

CLARENCE

Money for what?
Cille looks at him.
Never mind. I'll tell you what I'll do. I'll give you what I've got left: no questions asked.
*Holds out money to her. He leaves his coat
hanging on a chair.*
A little over two hundred dollars. Take it, and keep it.
Cille doesn't move.

CILLE

You've got three hundred. I looked in your wallet last night.

CLARENCE

Do you and Mama take turns going through my things? . . .
Stops. Laughs. Gives it to her.
I knew you wouldn't quit: you're still in the fight. I guess
I'm jealous. You're not fighting for me anymore.

CILLE

It's too late for you.
*Adelaide enters up left, wearing a tight black
raincoat. Walks to Riverview gates, looks in.
Then crosses quietly down to house.*

CLARENCE

What do you mean by that? Too late?

ADELAIDE
Calls.

Clarence.

CLARENCE
Turning.

What's that?

CELESTE
Entering down left.

Looky looky looky: if it ain't my favorite person to catch on
a Sunday morning. Miss Adelaide Smith.
*Adelaide turns and sees Celeste, but does not
flutter. Her manner has lost the frills, as have
her clothes. Instead of answering, she unbut-
tons and removes her coat to reveal a very
close-fitting, pure white dress. Walks to bench,
folds coat, sits on it.*
Wow. What happened to you? Look like you tripped into a
bottle of bleach water. What you doing, honey, getting
married or something?
Calls.

Cille.
Then to Clarence as he comes out.

She inside?

114

CLARENCE

Mama and Dan are waiting for you at the church, Adelaide.

ADELAIDE

I know they are, Clarence.

CLARENCE

You aren't going to meet them?

ADELAIDE

Yes, Clarence. After the crowd breaks up. I'm going to meet them.

CELESTE

To Cille as she comes out to gallery. Pointing at Adelaide.

What do you think of her? I ain't never seen Adelaide in nothing but black mourning clothes.

To Adelaide.

Don't they have white mourning someplace? Seems to me I heard they do. Georgia or someplace.

CLARENCE

Adelaide, they're waiting.

CELESTE

Looking up at the sky.

It ain't gonna rain; it's gonna slop. I can always predict about the weather. First off, see . . .

She gets no reaction.

Is anybody interested?

CLARENCE

We are . . . sure. *Adelaide's* got to *run.*

ADELAIDE

Looking at him for the first time.

Why no, Clarence. I came to see you. I'll be at church when the service is over. And I never run.

CELESTE

I can see a storm coming every time. I just hate to be alone when it rains.

CLARENCE
Deciding to ignore Adelaide and attend Celeste.
I thought you had a boy friend.

CELESTE
Him and me broke up.

CLARENCE
Low and deep: playing sex.
You'll find somebody else.

CELESTE
Course I will. Honey, if it started to flood, I might even make a grab for you.

CLARENCE
Glad to oblige a lady in a flood.

CELESTE
Don't lean all over me, sugar, you ain't my type on a dry day.

CLARENCE
I thought you said it was going to rain.

CELESTE
Giggling.
Not that hard. Well, I guess I'd better be going to the next service.
No one answers.
Cille, Dewey wants to know can he bring the flowers this afternoon? He's getting tired of the mornings. He . . .

CILLE
I don't know what's going to happen this afternoon.

CELESTE
Hurt.
That's nice; I'll tell him that.
To Adelaide.
And it is a sweet dress.
She exits.

ADELAIDE

Do you like it too, Clarence? It's the only one I saved in its natural color.

To Cille.

Cille, honey, would you run up into the cemetery and keep an eye on the church?

Cille exits.

CLARENCE

To Adelaide.

Say what you have to say.

ADELAIDE

So blunt? My.

CLARENCE

Adelaide, I'm in no mood for make-believe.

ADELAIDE

What a funny coincidence. That's just what I came to say.

CLARENCE

Then say it.

ADELAIDE

I'm in no mood for make-believe.

CLARENCE

Looking at his watch.

Adelaide, it's getting late. Just about the hour for me to . . .

ADELAIDE

It is already past the hour for you to tell me whether you are going to want me or not.

Quietly.

Am I blunt enough?

CLARENCE

I . . . don't get it.

ADELAIDE

You are about the only person left in town who doesn't. Except for your brother Daniel, and your mama: thanks to me.

117

And Clarence, I am worn out and tired. I have a friend in New York City named Howard Crawford. He's married, but he doesn't care. He has a great deal of money. Enough to take care of me.

CLARENCE

That's the most . . . You could just stand there . . . and say that?

ADELAIDE

I could stand here and say anything I had to say. I told you. I'm tired.

CLARENCE

Let's get this straight. Do I want you . . . *for what?*

ADELAIDE

The less the better as far as I'm concerned. But I wouldn't exactly care. Just so we got married.

CLARENCE

I don't think I'm hearing you right.

ADELAIDE

You haven't been hearing me right for years. It's about time you started.

CLARENCE

My God.

ADELAIDE

Don't take the Lord's name in vain, Clarence. Not on the Sabbath, and not in your mama's back yard. Have you got a cigarette?

CLARENCE

Have I got a what?

ADELAIDE

Wearily.
And don't shout. Have you got a simple cigarette?

118

CLARENCE

Not on me. You don't smoke.

ADELAIDE

Yes, I smoke.
          Sighs.
There. Now you know my horrible . . . shadiest secret.
          Slight pause. Hard.
I smoke.

CLARENCE

Adelaide, is this your way of being funny?

ADELAIDE

No, it's not. It's a shame if you don't know my ways of being
funny by now. I just ran out of them.

CLARENCE

It makes no sense. No sense at all. You walked over here today expecting I was going to marry you?

ADELAIDE

Matter of fact, I didn't, no. I don't expect you will.
          Carefully.
I just thought you ought to know how far I'd be willing to go.

CLARENCE

Just to marry me?

ADELAIDE

Don't puff up, sugar. Think.

CLARENCE

How long has it been this way?

ADELAIDE

Quite a long time, considering. Practically since the day you
came home with that phony telegram.
          As he starts to protest. Smiling.
It was the first thing that made me catch on to you, Clarence, the day you brought that home. I thought right then:
That boy will go far. And you did. Matter of fact, it was why

119

I let you walk me home that same night and . . . I believe the storybook way of saying it is Have Intimate Relations.

CLARENCE

That was a long time ago; we were just kids.

Suddenly embarrassed. Stammering like Dan.

My God . . . you're in love with me?

ADELAIDE

Bursts out laughing.

Nothing makes you untidy, does it? Love. You have such a neat mind, precious. I have always admired the neatness of your mind.

CLARENCE

Then you don't . . .

ADELAIDE

Of course I don't. I don't love anybody.

CLARENCE

But why . . .

ADELAIDE

Why what? I've been tired since three weeks ago when your mama took to inviting the neighbors in to see the side show. Walk right in, ladies and gentlemen. This is the house where dreams come true.

Laughs.

I don't plan to wait around for people like Celeste Chipley to come in and make fun of me. I don't even plan to wait for things like draft notices. Or for anything. It's time I was taken care of by somebody, my way.

Looks at him.

Somebody like you.

CLARENCE

Returning her look. Slowly.

You think I have money.

ADELAIDE

I got over thinking about things like money before I was weaned. I think about other things. I know about money.

CLARENCE
You're wrong. I don't have any. I just have a job.

ADELAIDE
I'm not wrong, I know you don't have any, and you don't
have a job either. I know where your money comes from. I
always did. And I know how much more there is where that
came from, and how many more people there are in the
world, like Mrs. Soren, or Miss Baker, or Mr. Stanley Woods.
Clarence rises.
Fact, I am acquainted with a few of them myself. Not many,
though. I'm too delicate for most of your clients. And I don't
work cheap.
Smiles.
I'm sorry I couldn't tell you sooner. The situation around
here would have been a little confusing if you'd known all
along.
Looks at him. Simply.
Now it's just a matter of plain fact. It seems your mama's
two favorite people are both whores.

CLARENCE
I don't believe you.
*Adelaide continues to stare at him. He backs
away and turns. A slight pause. Suddenly
whispers.*
Why can't you leave me alone? For God's sake why can't all
of you leave me alone?

ADELAIDE
You are too young to be left alone.

CLARENCE
I can't remember when I was young.

ADELAIDE
Smiles.
The Lover Boy of the World. You really think what you
do at night might shock somebody, and the only person on
earth it ever shocked was you.

121

CLARENCE

You say you're tired. You don't know what being tired means.

ADELAIDE

Don't I?

CLARENCE

Beginning to sound his age.

I can't remember once when I wanted to get up in the morning.

ADELAIDE

Oh that. And do you ever lie in your own bed and make believe you're not on this earth?

CLARENCE

Yes.

ADELAIDE

Softly.

And do you imagine there must be some other planet . . . some one place in the whole entire universe . . . with creature-things that don't have to make dreams out of their children?

Laughs.

Do you know what the first rocket ship is going to discover on the next world?

CLARENCE

What?

ADELAIDE

Big beetles showing little beetles what to do.

Clarence moves to the tree, his back turned.

If you want a different world . . .

CLARENCE

I don't want a different world. I would like to stay here and remember this one. I would like to remember how the sky smells. I wish I could sit still and think about that. I wish I could cry. If I'm so damn young, why can't I cry?

ADELAIDE

You don't really want to, do you?

CLARENCE

After a pause.

Will you please leave me alone?

ADELAIDE

Crosses to him. Kisses him. Clarence stands motionless. Simply.

Is that your best performance?

Clarence stands as if he were trying to focus his eyes. Then he takes Adelaide in his arms and kisses her, long and hard.

Clarence lets her go, turns his back.

Adelaide smiles.

Well?

CLARENCE

What am I supposed to do, turn around and tell you I love you?

ADELAIDE

Softly.

No indeed: you've never insulted me before. Why should you start now?

CLARENCE

Will you leave me in peace?

ADELAIDE

If that's what you want.

CLARENCE

What do you want? To be tired together?

ADELAIDE

No . . . No I don't. I don't think I ever wanted to be any-thing together. I don't even want to lay down in a feather bed . . . and do embroidery . . . crochet, like my mama did. I want to stand up and help somebody take care of me.

I will settle for Howard if I have to, but I don't prefer to. I prefer to settle for you. Because you are single; because you can make almost as much money as he has, if you are careful, and if somebody helps you to save what you make. Because, Clarence, you smell like money.

Kindly.

Sit down, precious, you're even beginning to look a little green.

Clarence sits.

I have this to offer to you. Only this, but it's important: I am the one woman you can marry that you wouldn't have to pretend for. I wouldn't care what you did, or who you did it with. Just so you never came home poor. I am beautiful: I can hold onto the cotton-candy world for you, sugar. I can protect you from your mama for the rest of time. I can be the same as you because we are the same. Orphans are like favorite babies. We never get a chance to learn how to love.

CLARENCE

After a pause. Slowly.

I never would have thought you hated so much.

ADELAIDE

I don't, storybook child. I don't hate so much. Only my mother's laying in bed . . . doing her fancy needlework for me to sell.

Very softly.

I never hated anything but needles.

Turning to him.

What is my answer, Clarence?

CLARENCE

What do you think it is?

ADELAIDE

I think it's no.

Clarence watches her.

It wouldn't be the army you're worried about? You can get out of that.

124

Smiles.

Just tell them one of your clients doesn't like men in uniform.

CLARENCE

Automatically.

I couldn't use any names.

ADELAIDE

You wouldn't have to. No names required. All you have to do is make a quiet pass at the inducting officer. He'll have a name.

A slight pause.

Or are you worried about your uncle, the deacon? I can get you free of him. I'm a capable girl, Clarence; I have an acquaintance downtown who takes care of making worms disappear.

A pause.

Is it still no?

Clarence stares at her.

Good luck, candyman. You might at least have stayed alive.

Dismisses him. Calls.

Cille.

CLARENCE

What do you want her for?

ADELAIDE

Nothing to do with you.

Kindly.

Why don't you run along and have a shot or two of liquor before your mama gets home?

Smiles.

You'll need it, Clarence . . . It's likely to be a jerky day.

Cille enters.

Honey, I have a request to make of you. About your *younger* brother . . . about . . .

CILLE

Dan.

ADELAIDE

Yes. I am leaving town. I don't want him following me.
Will you stop him, please?

CILLE

Slowly.

I don't know if I can.

ADELAIDE

You?

Simply.

Oh yes. You can.

CLARENCE

Stop him from what? What are . . .

ADELAIDE

Interrupting and ignoring him. To Cille.

I carried things a mite too far with Daniel. He thinks he's
my Guardian Angel, or something. He comes over at night
and stands on the stoop of my front gallery. For hours sometimes. He just watches my house.

CLARENCE

He what?

CILLE

Let her alone.

CLARENCE

That's enough. That's plenty enough. You've done enough
without making things up about Dan.

ADELAIDE

Making things up?

CLARENCE

Better catch hold now, while you can. It's not that serious
yet. We all do it, Adelaide. *We all dream.*

ADELAIDE

Do we?

126

Softly.

Yes, I suppose we do. We all dream about our mamas.

Quietly.

I dream about mine the way she was before she died: That whole last year when she lay in bed and called to me. I dream about telling her she had diabetes. Not cancer. Taking the money she'd saved and spending it on morphine so she wouldn't feel the pain. Doing what I did with the doctor to get as many prescriptions as she needed until she died . . . Yes. I dream.

Yells.

I dream about cash, not telegrams. And not about any man in this whole wide world, honey, would I dream. So you can stop thinking I would make up a story about your baby brother: while I was awake, or while I was asleep, or any kind of a way at all. I told you once all I want to do is live my life. Just get your brother out of it, will you, ché? Just get him the hell off my back.

CILLE

Reaching out to her. Gently.

This morning Dan said there was glass . . . growing inside of you. He said . . . it was like a garden . . .

ADELAIDE

Little Daniel said that? It ain't no garden, honey. Your family's got gardens on the brain. And it ain't glass.

CILLE

I know.

ADELAIDE

Do you? I didn't; not this time.

Picks up raincoat.

Not till a few weeks ago. I'm so tired of things growing in me I could throw up. And I'm more tired of having to do something about them. The last abortion made me sick to my stomach for a month. I guess I'm just tired.

Shrugs. Looks at herself vacantly in compact.

127

To Cille.
I used to have the feeling you could tell just about every time . . . couldn't you?

CILLE
I think you should always wear white.

ADELAIDE
Snaps compact shut. A short pause.
Is this a pretty compact?

CILLE
Yes.

ADELAIDE
Suddenly thrusting it at her. Hard.
Keep it. From New York City. I can't seem to hold a *heavy* compact. My hands are too delicate. Goodbye.
Stops by Clarence. To him.
Take care of everything. As they say.

CLARENCE
Adelaide, why didn't you let me see you before? You are beautiful.

ADELAIDE
Stares. Then whips him across the face with her raincoat.
God damn you for that.

CLARENCE
Stares at her.
Jesus, Jesus, Jesus . . .

DAN
Appearing at the gates.
Adelaide.

ADELAIDE
Yes, Daniel?

DAN
We was . . . waiting by the church. We . . .

128

ADELAIDE

Yes, indeed. I was just coming.

DAN

But . . .

*Mama enters gates. She stands at the center of
the yard. A pause.*

ADELAIDE

To Clarence.

I'm sorry she has to see me this way. I was going to put the
raincoat on, you see.

*Dan goes forward. Mama grabs him by the
shoulder, thrusts him back.*

I suppose it's too late now to do it the nice way. If there ever
really was a nice way.

A pause.

Well.

A pause.

Won't somebody say good morning?

MAMA

I will. Good morning.

ADELAIDE

And goodbye?

Smiles.

You're quite a woman, aren't you?

MAMA

Adelaide touches Clarence.

Cille exits to kitchen.

Him?

Slowly.

Has it been him all along . . . is that it?

ADELAIDE

Yes.

MAMA

You did your best to fool me all this time.

ADELAIDE

I didn't have to do my best. It was easy.

MAMA

Was it? For a bright girl . . . you're not very bright. You should have asked me a long time ago: I could have saved you a lot of waiting. I would never have let him settle for a . . . for a . . . whatever you are.

ADELAIDE

I'm another woman, Mrs. Morris.
Calls.
Sergeant Jameson . . . Sergeant Jameson.
A good-looking soldier in his thirties enters from left.

JAMESON

Yes, ma'am?

ADELAIDE

Sergeant Jameson has offered to drive me all the way up to New York City. I am going to be engaged when I get there. But not to him. Thank you for waiting. Are the suitcases in the car?

JAMESON

Yes, ma'am.

ADELAIDE

I didn't expect to be so long. It seems I am going with you after all.

JAMESON

Well, come on, honey . . .

ADELAIDE

Not "honey," no. I do think from *ma'am* to *honey* is a bit too sudden, don't you?
He starts toward her. She pushes her raincoat at him.
I should say . . . "Miss Smith" . . . for the first fifty miles. After that you're on your own.

She runs out. He follows.

There is a pause.

DAN

Adelaide . . .

MAMA

Keep back.

A pause. To Clarence, low.

What have you been doing?

He doesn't answer. Mama takes a breath and says.

What have you been doing with her?

CLARENCE

Mama, I . . .

MAMA

Don't try to lie now.

CLARENCE

I . . . I couldn't even see . . . what she was like . . . until . . .

MAMA

Liar.

CLARENCE

Dan, wait . . . It's not my fault she was pretending . . .

MAMA

Whose fault is it? Whose?

DAN

A slight pause.

Yours, Mama.

MAMA

Coming toward him.

Daniel baby . . . Daniel . . .

Dan spits in her face. Mama rocks back against the house. Dan runs once to the tree and back, like a broken mechanical toy, and runs out

*the Riverview gates. Inside the kitchen, Cille
sits. From the house next door the radio blasts
out jazz.*

Daniel will come back to me.

CLARENCE

Of course he will, Mama.
Shouts.
Turn that radio down.
*Clarence starts to go to Mama. She turns and
goes in the house. Clarence follows her.*

MAMA
Suddenly unable to look at Cille.
Get her out of here. Take her inside.

CILLE

I won't go, Mama.

MAMA

Give her her medicine.

CILLE

I won't take it. I don't need it.

MAMA

Get her away, I said. Put a pillow on her eyes.
Clarence takes Cille off.

Turns out light.
That bruise-colored sky is seeping right down into my
kitchen.
Calls.
You lied to me about Adelaide. What else did you lie about?
To herself.
God help me. Somebody help me to understand. I don't
understand: I come from Atlanta. My soft light. At the end
of the day. What soft light?
Loud.
I come from Atlanta.
Stops short, remembering something. Reaches

132

in pocket of Clarence's jacket lying on chair.
Takes out letter. Unfolds and looks at it.
Glances at telegram. Then says, slowly.
"Government of the United States . . ."
She crumples the letter. Sits in the rocker. A
pause.

The kitchen is now filled with the dead,
bloated gray light of the sky. It is as if one
enormous, unbroken shadow had descended:
the storm sits, swollen between earth and sky,
over the house and the two graveyards. The
silence grows.

Clarence enters. He moves without sound, as
he has throughout the play, pausing to close
the living-room door, then padding softly in-
side. Clarence's step is not light. He moves to
where Mama is sitting, and stands directly
behind her.

Mama sits without moving, the letter hidden
in her lap. She becomes uneasily aware that
Clarence is standing behind her, but does not
turn around. For most of the following scene
the voices are kept unusually low, always
conscious of Cille's presence in the next room.
The emotions must be communicated with
the least possible quantity of sound. They be-
gin almost in whispers.
I didn't see nothing this time.
A slight pause.
Not even your shadow.

CLARENCE
It's dark in here.

MAMA
I turned out the light.

CLARENCE

She wouldn't take the medicine, Mama. She said she'd go to
sleep without it. She's almost asleep now.

Mama doesn't answer.

I think I'd better go and . . .

MAMA

Holds up letter.

First you will want to tell me about your draft notice. That's
what the letter is. Ain't it?

CLARENCE

*Sucks his breath in; draws back as though the
paper were on fire.*

Put it back.

MAMA

Still facing front.

Take it.

CLARENCE

It belongs to me.

MAMA

Then take it. I don't want it.

Reaches behind her, drops it on table.

I matched it to the words in my telegram. You taught me
them words. I know what it is, thanks to you.

CLARENCE

I never liked your thanks.

MAMA

You lied to me . . . about the sweepstakes . . . about everything . . . you make the world a lie.

CLARENCE

Wasn't that the way you wanted it, Mama?

MAMA

Everything you touch.

134

CLARENCE

Everything?

MAMA

All the things but one. Only my telegram. That's all I got
left now. Why didn't you tell me you was going in the army?

CLARENCE

Because I'm not sure yet whether I'm going in or not.

MAMA

Then I will teach you.
        Rises.
Because I'm sure.
                *Turns to him. Clarence sees the look on her
                face, and moves quickly toward the living
                room.*
You can't go in there, your sister's in there.
                He starts for his bedroom.
Or there either. You can't go any place at all till I get
through with you.

CLARENCE

You are already through with me.

MAMA

Not yet: no. Do you think you're too good for the army?
                Points to telegram.
Are you any better than that up there?

CLARENCE

        Slowly.
Yes, Mama. Of course. I am better than that up there . . .
                Mama slaps him gently across the mouth.
                A pause.

MAMA

What are you planning? to follow after her?

CLARENCE

I might be.

135

MAMA

Oh no you're not. Do you know what that girl is?

CLARENCE

Yes, Mama. I know what she is. And I would rather live with
her than live with you.

> *She slaps him again, involuntarily and much
> harder.*

MAMA

I don't understand you, Clarence. *What are you?*

CLARENCE

A hustler.

MAMA

What?

CLARENCE

You heard me, Mama. You know what a hustler is.

MAMA

No.

CLARENCE

Oh, yes, you do. The man they caught and beat all over his
body with a big sack of wood.

MAMA

I don't . . . I don't remember anything about that . . .

CLARENCE

> *Unbuttoning his shirt.*

Look at me, Mama.

> *He turns on the light.*

Now look.

> *He rips his shirt off and stands facing her,
> naked to the waist and holding his arms out
> so that she can see. There are bruise marks on
> his neck and chest. His shoulders are purple
> and black.*

MAMA
Looks at him. Count five. Dully.
I knew when they pulled you from my body that you were
going to die. I hope you die soon.
Turns to wall.
There it is. The dirty shadow: there it is.
Speaks to the shadow.
You get out of my house now. And don't ever come back.
You're infecting all my children.
Clarence crosses toward door.
Wait.
She turns slowly to face him.
First, I want to know. Did you lie to me about everything?
About that up there?
He does not answer.
Bring it here.

CLARENCE
Brings the telegram to her.
What do you want me to do, Mama?

MAMA
I want to know the truth.

CLARENCE
Now?

MAMA
Right now.

*Unable to answer her, Clarence lifts, then
smashes the telegram down against the corner
of the table. The glass shatters in all directions
as the wood corner goes through; he drops the
frame to the floor.*

*Mama opens her mouth and gives one long,
agonized, voiceless scream. Then she grabs her
belly as if her pain had become localized, and
buckles suddenly into the rocking chair. Clarence backs away from her, looking like a film*

137

shown in reverse. As he passes the table he hesitates just long enough to pick up the letter and his shirt. Then he backs out the door; turns, glides across the yard through the cemetery gates, and is gone.

CILLE
Enters from living room.

Mama . . . What was . . .

She sees the telegram. Stoops. Touches it. Hears neighbors—goes outside.

Two people run on from left. They stand looking up at the house, whispering. Cille hears them and puts frame down and goes out to gallery as Deacon Sittre comes on left.

To the people.

Don't whisper here.

WOMAN

But, honey . . . we heard a noise. We're your new neighbors; from over there. We was just wondering . . .

CILLE

Wonder what you want. But don't whisper here. It was my mama who screamed. She screamed because she happened to feel like it.

They draw back. Celeste enters.

Just go home. And don't whisper here.

The two neighbors exit. Deacon Sittre comes forward and starts up steps.

You get out too.

He stops.

Did you hear me?

He hesitates. Almost with Mama's voice, but with a difference, Cille shouts in his face.

I said you get out too.

He backs away from her and exits.

CELESTE
Entering, to her.

Hey, honey, take it easy . . . You don't want them new neighbors to think you're mean.

CILLE

Why not? Up to now they thought I was peculiar.

CELESTE
Looks at her.

Hey, you look better. You . . . been looking odd lately.
Tapping her own head.
Like you was going to get another . . .

CILLE
Slowly.

I don't think there'll be any more headaches.

CELESTE

Listen to the good news.
Points up.
Hey, look. Look at the moon in the morning. It's clearing.

DEWEY
Entering with flowers.

What happened?

CELESTE

Nothing happened. Mrs. Morris just had a little upset.

DEWEY

Oh. I brought her the flowers for the . . .

CILLE

She doesn't need any more flowers.

DEWEY
A pause.

She . . . don't?
Staring at her. Holds flowers out. Slowly.
Well then maybe *you* . . .
Cille reaches out. She takes them.

CELESTE
To Dewey.

Come on, honey. You can come back and see her tomorrow.
Come on.

> *She leads Dewey forcibly off by the hand.*
> *Cille goes back into house. Mama is sitting*
> *exactly as before.*

MAMA

You just told them to leave. I heard you.

CILLE

Yes, Mama.

MAMA

Them people been whispering around this house for years.
Ever since Clarence was born. You just told them to stop.
And they did.

CILLE

Yes.

MAMA

Now tell me. It ain't true. Is it? About George?

CILLE

No, Mama. It's not true.

MAMA

Where is he?

CILLE

In jail.

MAMA
After a slight pause. Echoes.

Jail.

CILLE

He killed somebody. Clarence made you the telegram when
he found out. He did it . . . because . . .

MAMA
Flat.

Because it was the only thing I wanted then.

140

CILLE

Yes. And . . .

MAMA

I think you'd better clean up that mess on the floor.

Dan enters from Riverview gates. Walks to kitchen door. Comes in.

DAN

Mama, I . . .

MAMA

Who is that?

DAN

It's me, Mama. I . . .

MAMA

Hard. Ordering.

Stand where you are. Lucille, do we have any money in the house?

CILLE

For what?

MAMA

I want him to leave.

CILLE

We . . .

Slowly.

I have three hundred dollars. I was going to give it to him . . . so he could get away.

MAMA

After a short pause.

Then give it to him.

DAN

Scared.

Mama, I . . .

MAMA

I do not want him around me. Ever. He spit in my face. I

141

want him to leave. Which train would you of told him to take?

Mama, please. I ain't going no place, I . . .

MAMA
Lucille.

CILLE
Yes.

MAMA
Shut your brother's mouth.

DAN
I won't, I won't shut up. Mama, please. I ain't got no place to go. Mama, I passed Clarence on the other side of the cemetery. He's . . . He was on his way to the Induction Center. He said he was going in . . . five days early . . . Mama . . . and he's asking to be sent overseas right away. He wants to get in on the fighting quick before the war is over. He even said . . .

MAMA
It don't matter what he said.
        A slight pause.
It don't matter.

DAN
But I been thinking. It wasn't your fault . . . about Adelaide, and . . .

MAMA
It was my fault. Certainly it was. You are stupid.

DAN
Mama . . . I'm sorry I spit . . .

MAMA
        Strong.
Lucille, I asked you which train was you going to make him take.

142

CILLE
Quietly. Still looking at her. Puzzled.
The six o'clock train, Mama.

MAMA
Why that train?

CILLE
It's the only train I knew about. It goes to Atlanta. I knew because . . .

MAMA
Because I used to tell you about it. In all them bedtime stories. Six o'clock was the hour when everything changed to something beautiful . . .

CILLE
Yes.

DAN
Mama . . .

MAMA
Then tell him to take that train. To forget about her. And go to Atlanta.
There is a short pause.
Was you going to give him anything else?

CILLE
The gold watch Clarence gave me. It must be worth another twenty.

DAN
Runs to her. Weeping.
No. Mama, *please* . . .

MAMA
Don't touch me. Get away from me. I don't want you.
Carefully.
You are the stupidest one of all my children.
More carefully.
I never did want you.
Dan turns away.

DAN

But . . . you was always . . .

MAMA

I was always only pretending.

DAN

Tremulous; stammering.

But . . . what would I do in Atlanta? Mama . . . we ain't got no more family there . . . I might not get a job. Supposing . . . I might . . . starve, I . . .

MAMA

That is a chance you will have to take. Get out and act like a man.

CILLE

Mama . . .

MAMA

Get out.

> Cille hands him money and watch. A slight pause.

DAN

I won't starve, Mama. No matter what you say.

> Dan moves slowly away from her. Turns to Cille. Walks rigidly out to yard. There is a pause.

MAMA

Watch for him.

CILLE

Mama.

MAMA

Watch him now.

> Cille looks out screen door. Dan is seen walking slowly along the cemetery wall. He stops for a second by the gates; then continues past them and exits up left.

How did he go?

144

CILLE

The right way, Mama. Past the cemetery, to the railroad station.

MAMA

That's good.

CILLE
Crosses to her.
You didn't mean any of that. You lied to him just now.

MAMA
Still facing front; not moving.
Of course.

CILLE

You weren't angry because he spit . . .

MAMA

No. I wasn't angry. He believed me, though. My sons are like me: they believe when people lie. My sons lie all the time.

CILLE

But why did you do it?

MAMA

Why? I just found out. It's not safe around me.

CILLE

Mama, is Clarence coming back?

MAMA

No. This is your house now. We finished all the payments on it, him and me. He wouldn't come back to your house.

CILLE

Mama . . . what went on while I was asleep?
Shaking her head.
Clarence . . . went in the army? Five days early?
A slight pause.
I don't understand why he would do that.

MAMA

I do.

Before Cille can answer.

Now. I would like to have them pieces of glass down there.

CILLE

Looks at floor. Gently.

You don't want that. It's just broken glass, Mama.

Picks up silver frame, shakes it out.

Here. You can have this.

MAMA

Takes frame obediently without looking. Holds it in her lap.

Sweep it up then. You clean up the mess.

A slight pause.

Clarence was my favorite baby.

Rocking. Shyly.

I never told him that.

CILLE

Please hush.

Takes broom, begins to sweep up glass.

MAMA

Daniel is going all by himself to Atlanta. It was the place for him to go. Atlanta.

CILLE

I know, Mama.

MAMA

I loved all my babies, all of them. Did you know that?

CILLE

Yes.

MAMA

Unconsciously takes the empty frame in her arms as though it were an infant. Rocking the frame.

I rocked all my babies in this chair.

Stops the movement abruptly with her feet.

146

But that's all over. I don't want to rock any more. Once when I was a girl . . . a girl your age . . . they brought me a doll. My papa brought it. I was too old for a doll. But I had always wanted one before. Ain't it funny the way they bring you the things you want when you don't want them? Ain't it funny?

Frowning suddenly.

What will we do now?

CILLE

I love you. We'll get along, Mama. Please . . .

MAMA

Get along? Us? You know you are the only child I never understood: and *we'll* get along? I want Clarence. Where has Clarence gone? Don't you really know?

A slight pause. Guttural.

He went to get me a real telegram. With his name on it. For this here frame. That's what he did. And I don't want it. I don't want to wait for it.

Leans forward. Calls loud.

I don't want a *real* telegram.

CILLE

Backing away from her slowly. Whispers.

Mama . . . Clarence couldn't have gone in the army just to get himself killed . . .

MAMA

Couldn't he? My twilight. I wish you could of seen his body. *What twilight?*

CILLE

But Clarence . . .

MAMA

What Clarence?

CILLE

A whispered scream.

Mama . . .

MAMA

Carefully. Flat.

Hush, now, hush. There's nothing to do about it now. Just
listen to the sky clear. We won't even have to work: he
took care of that too. Listen, now: listen to the wind.

*Cille stands, frozen with horror. Mama begins
to rock the frame again back and forth in the
chair.*

*For a count of five. Then very slowly, as a
person moving in a dream, Cille walks to
Mama's chair, and puts a hand on her shoulder. Mama continues to rock until—*

CURTAIN

About the Author

PETER S. FEIBLEMAN was born in New York City in 1930 and spent his childhood in the New Orleans that provides the setting for this play. A student of drama at the Carnegie Institute of Technology and at Columbia University, Mr. Feibleman has more than a passing acquaintance with the theater. From 1951 to 1958 he lived in Spain working as an actor and as the manager of a Spanish ballet company which toured Europe and North Africa. It was also in Spain that he completed his first novel, *A Place Without Twilight*, published in 1958, which received much critical acclaim. A second novel, *Daughters of Necessity*, followed in 1959. Mr. Feibleman now resides in New York where he is at work on a new play, as yet untitled, and on a new novel, *Strangers and Graves*.

This book was set in

Caledonia and Deepdene types,

printed, and bound by

Doubleday and Company, Inc.

Design is by Larry Kamp.